the
whole
life

the
whole
life

FINDING GOD'S RHYTHM FOR
YOUR SPIRIT, SOUL, AND BODY

DAVID STINE

HOWARD BOOKS
New York   London   Toronto   Sydney   New Delhi

Howard Books
An Imprint of Simon & Schuster, Inc.
1230 Avenue of the Americas
New York, NY 10020

First Howard Books hardcover edition January 2019

HOWARD and colophon are trademarks of Simon & Schuster, Inc.

For information about special discounts for bulk purchases, please contact Simon & Schuster Special Sales at 1-866-506-1949 or business@simonandschuster.com.

The Simon & Schuster Speakers Bureau can bring authors to your live event. For more information or to book an event, contact the Simon & Schuster Speakers Bureau at 1-866-248-3049 or visit our website at www.simonspeakers.com.

Medical Disclaimer:
This book contains general information about nutrition and fitness. The information is not professional medical advice, and should not be treated as such.

> If you have any specific questions about any nutrition- or fitness-related issue addressed in this book you should consult your doctor or other professional healthcare provider.

> If you think you may be suffering from any medical condition you should seek immediate medical attention.

> You should never delay seeking medical advice, disregard medical advice, or discontinue medical treatment because of information in this book.

> Nothing in this medical disclaimer will limit any of our liabilities in any way that is not permitted under applicable law, or exclude any of our liabilities that may not be excluded under applicable law.

Interior design by Davina Mock-Maniscalco
Illustrations by Becka Gruber and Richard Matthews

Manufactured in the United States of America

10 9 8 7 6 5 4 3 2 1

Library of Congress Cataloging-in-Publication Data is available.

ISBN 978-1-5011-5190-3
ISBN 978-1-5011-5191-0 (ebook)

To my children:
Isaac, Josiah, Asher, and Karis

Contents

Introduction

I felt like a well that had run dry. As a pastor of a growing multisite church, I had focused solely on being the spiritual man of God that my role demanded, to the detriment of my emotional health and physical well-being—and it wasn't working! I taught, led, and counseled others out of an overflow of my relationship with God, but—combined with the other demands of my job and my family—I was facing a frightening burnout. I had absolutely nothing more to give.

My marriage was not in a good place even before I reached this point. I had been absent from too much of the early lives of my four children. At the same time I had to face some serious health issues. Presented with a long list of stressors and broken situations, I clearly understood that my role at the church was at the root of everything I was dealing with.

Ten years prior, my wife, Taryn, and I felt called to the D.C. metropolitan area. With our first son just an infant and a second on the way, we moved from Jacksonville, Florida, where we had both flourished on the staff of a large multisite church there as well. God had given me a vision to plant multiple churches in and around the D.C. metro area. This became our mission field.

Upon moving to the area, we chose to base our church in Alexandria, Virginia, and start the work God put on our hearts in a Regal movie theater. We felt if we could reach D.C., serving those who work tirelessly to serve our country, we could reach the rest of the country. Ten years later, D.C. Metro Church was well on its way to becoming the multisite church we had dreamed of. We offered nine weekend services between our three locations in Alexandria, Fairfax, and Woodbridge, with plans for even more expansion on the drawing board. With a large paid staff, a volunteer team of around eight hundred, and a membership quickly approaching six thousand, the load had become a heavy burden.

Shepherding members and staff through crisis after crisis, with the ever-present financial needs of a large, growing organization hanging over my head, I had attempted to step away from the stress for short seasons during the prior three years. I took multiple retreats and an extended sabbatical, but I still felt just as empty and disconnected—and, I found myself even *more* frustrated after my times away. I'd done everything I knew to do—prayed harder and longer, quoted Scripture—but nothing was different. Nothing inside me had changed after each futile effort. I tried to mask the growing disappointment I felt with sheer determination, but inwardly I was losing hope and growing disillusioned that my situation could be beyond help.

———

In January of 2017, after going in for what I thought was a routine physical, my doctor confronted me, asking what was going on in my life. He shared with me that my blood pressure was not looking good and my heart rate was an active 115 beats per minute in a calm, rested state. After a brief conversation about my stress levels, coffee intake, and poor sleep habits—I was averaging only two hours of sleep per night—he ordered a giant battery of blood work, which revealed that I had an extremely hyperactive thyroid.

My thyroid hormone release levels were off the charts. He estimated my metabolism was revving eight times higher than what it should have been. His recommendation was to immediately remove all the stressors from my life. I was also prescribed medicine to regulate my heart rate until he could figure out what was wrong with me. A few days later I went back to the doctor and was diagnosed by a specialist as having an autoimmune hyperthyroid disorder called Graves' disease. Surprisingly, I learned I'd had this disease my entire life. The doctor said patients usually only find out they have it when under extremely stressful situations that trigger and sustain an overactive thyroid gland. Added to this, the doctor recommended I visit a psychiatrist, where I was additionally diagnosed with PTSD from the constant crisis in the church combined with my undiagnosed Graves'.

A pastor of a large multisite church often wears three hats: a CEO; a private, contemplative writer of sermons; and a public inspirational speaker. I needed to be the well-organized businessman and administrator in the boardroom; a deeply theological spiritual authority with a well-reviewed and completely original message every week; and also a lighthearted comedian and encourager. I went from the agony of trauma in the life a church member, to the excitement over a young couple getting married, to meetings where I faced that we were millions of dollars in the hole—then had to be gregarious and spiritually insightful on the weekends; I felt like I lived my life battling a rollercoaster ride of emotions. It was clear that this job description was more than my capabilities could handle in my burned-out state, and I began to realize that this wild ride had to come to an end, or I would.

On February 2, I delivered what was to be my final sermon at the church, titled "How to Survive a Shipwreck," taken from Acts 27. Paul was shipwrecked on the isle of Malta. Paul knew the shipwreck was inevitable but that God would be with him in the process. Even though the ship was destroyed, Paul and his crew made it ashore on the pieces of the ship. Although I didn't choose the passage for this purpose, looking back later on I felt like it was a fitting farewell and coincidental conclusion of what I had been going through privately for well over a year.

Even though I did not know that I was officially leaving at that moment, I was convinced that *I* was the thing that needed to change. After delivering the message that night and walking back to my seat, I had a feeling that it would be my last for some time. I didn't return to the church again. The next day the church overseers asked me to stay home, as they were aware that I was dealing with a serious thyroid condition. Shortly after this diagnosis, I was asked to go on an indefinite leave of absence in order to get well. I was given an opportunity to say good-bye to the church I had founded ten years prior, during the weekend services. This may have been the single hardest thing that I had to do in my decade at the church. In April, while in and out of the doctor's office, hospital, and the psychiatrist's—I decided to resign.

THE EARLY DAYS

I wanted to recapture that passion and energy I had when I was just starting out, and I was so desperate to find it. Was there something that I had missed? I felt like maybe there was a required class on "maintaining your joy" that I had somehow forgotten to take. I wondered if it was possible for any of us to live our whole lives with passion and energy, or if the feeling was simply limited to our younger years.

When I first came to Christ, I never dreamed of being a pastor of a large multisite church in our nation's capital. But I always felt like I was called for something. I could never truly shake my desire to simply experience more of what Jesus offered and spoke of in the book of John, chapter ten, where He states the reason He came to earth in the first place, "that they might have life, and that they might have it more abundantly" (KJV). I was basically obsessed with Jesus and the attributes of the Christian life that He promised within the four Gospels, and I desired that others experience these same truths.

In those first ten to fifteen years of following Jesus, my life seemed truly amazing to me, like I had found a hidden mystery of this ethereal life as I followed Christ into every decision and became a student of God's Word and of pious prayer. I even gave up a promising career with a department store chain's headquarters to work with young people at a local church. Don't get me wrong: My life was not perfect or without problems; but with my connection to Jesus, I felt like there was nothing that could stop the plan of God from unfolding in my life. I saw many miracles in my early days of ministry, mostly with young people. I also took notice of how others felt that these happenings were abnormal for someone who hadn't given his life to Christ until he was twenty-one years old. Yet, all these things seemed very normal to me as I studied the book of Acts and the Epistles. In fact, it seemed abnormal outside of my readings that they were not happening more often in the church as a whole. In my novice mind this had become quite a conundrum.

As I began to make strides in my own walk with Christ, it seemed that becoming a pastor was the obvious next step for me—it felt like the next level in this newfound life that I had discovered. Early on, my father challenged me: "If you are going to do this the right way, then maybe you should get a professional degree for it." His words have always resonated deeply with me, and I had started to feel like I could use some real training, as my degree in business, although very helpful later on, was not helping me much with the greater theological issues I wanted to tackle, like God's will for my life.

At age twenty-five, I was looking at two different opportunities: one in Nashville, Tennessee, to learn the Christian music industry as an agent for Christian bands; and another to attend the seminary at Regent University in Virginia Beach, Virginia. Dad and I prayed that God would make the right choice crystal clear for me. It felt like a real fork in the road of my life. We asked that God would reveal the right path for me in the next ten days. A couple days later I received a phone call from the admissions office at Regent University offering me a full scholarship, which I promptly accepted. Several years and two degrees later, I emerged ready to start my journey as a pastor. I didn't anticipate where that path would lead me, or that here I would end up finding the answers to the problems that would later overwhelm me long before my burned-out future self would need them.

THE EPIPHANY

While in seminary, I wrote my doctoral dissertation on 1 Thessalonians 5:23–24. It is the benediction, or blessing, at the end of Paul's letter to the members of the church at Thessaloniki, whom he challenged to love others and commit to lives of holiness in light of the second coming of Christ. "And the very God of peace sanctify you wholly; and I pray God your whole spirit and soul and body be preserved blameless unto the coming of our Lord Jesus Christ. Faithful is he that calleth you, who also will do it" (KJV).

In that passage, the word *wholly* in the Greek language means full in each part or the ability to fill parts. Reading further in the passage, we find that the filled parts are the three interconnected parts of a human: spirit, soul, and body. This word, translated in English as *wholly*, was commonly used in the culture of the time, but only used in the Bible here in Thessalonians. Paul chose a term that was commonly understood by the reader as a setup for understanding the three parts of man.

The word *whole* in 1 Thessalonians 5:23–24 is *holokleros*. In the Greek, the first part of the word *holos* means whole, or sound; and *kleros* means properly apportioned in each part. It occurs only one other time in the New Testament in James 1:4 where it talks about being complete, lacking nothing. So *holokleros* can be defined by combining the two definitions as *a sound lifestyle pattern that is properly apportioned.*

In the English language we often talk about rhythm, a sound with regular repeated movement, when referring to a balanced life. A Whole Life rhythm is therefore *a sound lifestyle pattern that yields divine wholeness*. Based on this understanding of the Greek text, I've rewritten 1 Thessalonians 5:23–24 below:

And the very God of peace sanctify you fully in each part, and I pray that God would give you a Whole Life rhythm in your spirit, soul, and body without blame at the coming of our Lord Jesus Christ. Faithful is He that calls you, He will also help you to find your unique Whole Life rhythm.

During the crisis and stress I was facing, I remembered my dissertation topic and the profound truths I had studied in 1 Thessalonians 5:23–24. My thought was if I could somehow experience the balance I had written about, where there were established rhythms in my life, I would not only recover from burnout but also begin to thrive again. I had studied the concept in theory but needed to get to a place where I could actually practice what I knew to be true from God's Word.

As I meditated on that passage, I began to understand that these rhythms were exactly what I was missing in my relationship with my family, with God, even with myself. I needed to sort out my priorities, change my role in the church, and figure out a way to bring my life in line with God's plan for me—and for all believers. Once God had gracefully led me to this conclusion, I was able to fully embrace the principles that I knew to be true from this passage, which solidified my first epiphany: *Each of us can achieve personal wholeness by focusing on finding rhythm in our three parts: spirit, soul, and body.*

The other epiphany in 1 Thessalonians 5:23–24 comes at the end of verse 24 where it states that *God will help me to find my unique Whole Life rhythm*. Not only was scripture identifying what was missing in my life, but I was reassured that God Himself was going to help me find my unique rhythm.

FACING THE TRUTH

Recognizing just how out of sync my life was, I quickly committed to doing whatever it took to get back to peak health. After only a few weeks of focusing on my soul in therapy and my body through diet, exercise, and medical consultation, I felt a marked difference in my life. Once my soul and body started regaining health, my spiritual vitality rebounded, too. It was then, and is still today, amazing to realize how focusing on all three areas instead of just one brought about unprecedented health and fulfillment to my life.

Shortly after revisiting those life-changing words in 1 Thessalonians 5:23–24, I found myself on a fishing trip off the coast of Key West with some pastor friends. I shared what I had recently rediscovered about the Whole Life rhythm with my friend Rob Hoskins, the founder of OneHope and chairman of the board of directors at Oral Roberts University. He shared with me that ORU's mission statement actually comes from 1 Thessalonians 5:23, "to build Holy Spirit–empowered leaders through whole person education to impact the world with God's healing." Rob told me that at ORU they intentionally try to help the students focus on health and wholeness in their spirit, soul, and body. When I asked Rob what book he recommended to the students to practically apply 1 Thessalonians 5:23 to their lives, he said he didn't know of one.

That conversation with Rob was my confirmation to write this book to help others apply Whole Life principles to their lives in a practical way. If I was able to find God's rhythm for my spirit, soul, and body, you can, too. Your needs and challenges may or may not be as extreme as mine were, but by taking stock of all three parts of your life and identifying where you are on the journey toward wholeness, you can evaluate and assess what changes need to be made and experience the same amazing results as I did: balanced emotions, clarity in your mind, strength in your body, and a reinvigorated relationship with God. In other words, a life lived whole!

one

A Life Lived Whole

We were created to be expressions
of the goodness and wholeness of God.
—Erwin McManus

Jesus saith unto him, Rise, take up thy bed, and walk.
And immediately the man was made whole...
—John 5:8–9[1]

In the eclectic Del Ray neighborhood in Alexandria, Virginia, fitness studios were on every block. One day as I drove home with my then eight-year-old son Josiah, we passed by a hot-yoga studio. The traffic was slow enough that Josiah was able to get a good look through the front window of the studio. I noticed a quizzical expression on his face as he tried to figure out what those women were doing inside. I have often wondered the same thing and was quite curious what he was thinking about the women who were sweating and twisted in apparent pain.

Josiah asked, "Daddy, why are those ladies eating hot yogurt?" I laughed at his obvious misreading of the sign. I explained that the women were working out in a really hot room to try to get in shape. You could tell the concept seemed quite odd to him, and if I am honest, I was a little baffled by it, too. However, what stood out to me the most was that the sign right below *Hot Yoga* read: *Body, Mind, Spirit.*

I started thinking how many times I had seen that same phrase *body, mind, spirit* at some of the other yoga studios around town, on book covers, and at many spiritual wellness centers. I was intrigued that they'd clearly recognized that humans consisted of three inter-connected parts that needed equal care and attention. In stark contrast, many churches I was familiar with—even my own—only focused on the spiritual dimension of a person and did very little to encourage members' holistic growth. It was a truth that I was beginning to understand from a biblical perspective in my own life.

FINDING TRUTH

Growing up in a Catholic home, I had what I'd consider a secondhand knowledge of God during childhood. My understanding of God didn't come from personal experience but from the experiences of others—in my case, my parents and grandparents. Because I had no real personal experience of God, there wasn't a meaningful connection between the two of us.

As a young boy, in an attempt to get to know God, I became an altar boy. The problem was I wasn't a very good one: I could never remember when to ring the bells during the service. Whenever I showed up to put on my robe before Sunday mass, the priest would roll his eyes, knowing there would be a pregnant pause between his words and my dawning realization each time I was to ring the bells.

My sister and I attended church on Saturday nights when we were old enough to go without our parents. We chose Saturday night because the service was usually fifteen minutes shorter than Sunday. Even so, I often ended up dozing off in the middle of service, including once yelling out loudly as the result of a bad dream. My poor sister was mortified as everyone in the sanctuary turned and looked at us. Since church at that time wasn't cutting it for me, I began searching for truth outside of the church. I wanted to find answers to the bigger questions about the meaning of life—and I was willing to look anywhere that might have answers.

As a teenager, I did not understand about how to submit my life to God. I knew the stories but was confused about where *I* fit in to the whole equation. For me, there was a God, and my parents, grandparents and others around me were very excited about Him, but I was still trying to find Him on my own. By the time I was in college, I was an avid reader of self-help books and then New Age books: astrology, numerology, and even New Age prophecy. The essence of self-help philosophy and the New Age movement is similar: Everything you need is found inside you.

At the time, I read *The Power of Positive Thinking*, as the theme seemed to fit right into my self-help mentality. What I didn't know when I picked up the book is that the author, Norman Vincent Peale, presented more than another self-help philosophy. He used Scripture and included a salvation prayer for the reader at the end. I enjoyed the book so much, I read it four times within weeks of picking it up. It was Peale's use of Scripture that prepared me for my eventual reading of the Bible.

I finally stumbled upon the truth I was looking for in the most unexpected of ways. My parents were flying into Salt Lake City to join me for a skiing trip. As I waited for their arrival at the airport, a friendly older man offered me a pocket-sized orange Gideon Bible made up of the New Testament, Psalms, and Proverbs. I was familiar with Chinese proverbs, so I started reading the book of Proverbs on the ski trip. Within the next week I had finished all thirty-two chapters. I was amazed at the depth of wisdom on those small pages in Proverbs; the book contained the wisdom I had been lacking at that point in my life. That was the beginning of my journey toward God. After reading the four Gospels and the book of Acts, I clearly realized that His Word was the truth I had been looking for all along.

One truth that changed my life was Jesus' claim that He is the way, the truth, and the life, and that no man comes to the Father except through Him. I had recently read C. S. Lewis's thoughts that Jesus was either a liar, a lunatic, or Lord. Jesus was a great teacher, healer, leader, and prophet, but He claimed to be the Lord—God in the flesh.

Lewis felt it was foolish to accept Jesus as a great moral teacher yet refuse the claim that He is God.[2] As I read His Word, it actually made sense to me, and I found myself agreeing with Lewis that if He was not the Lord, by His own words He was a liar and lunatic—and one of the greatest con men who ever lived, based on the millions who have followed Him throughout history.

As I submitted to Him as Lord over my life, accepting Him as the only way to the Father, I recognized that I could not mix my hodge-podge of New Age ideas and practices with Christianity.

SPIRIT, SOUL, AND BODY

What captured my attention with the sign at the hot-yoga studio was not just the awareness that they understood the three parts of a human but that they had the order reversed from what God had laid out through Paul in 1 Thessalonians 5:23.

There is a biblical principle often referred to as the Law of First Mention. Simply stated, the first time something is mentioned in the Bible—or the order in which ideas are mentioned—sets the theological foundation for all future mentions of that theme. In 1 Thessalonians 5:23, the order is spirit, soul, and body.

For the purposes of this book, *spirit* refers to our human spirit, which gives us our consciousness of God and through which the Holy Spirit draws us closer to a lifestyle that reflects our eternal destination of heaven and its Prince of Peace. The Greek word for spirit is *pneuma*, meaning the spirit of a person. The spiritual formation section of this book focuses on the three main practical areas that draw us closer in communion with God: prayer, Bible study, and creating a God-sized dream.

Soul, as used in this book, refers to the personality of a human that originates from the word *psyche*, the Greek word for soul. This part of a person lives forever. The soul care section of this book focuses on the three parts of the soul—the mind, the will, and emotions—and gives practical advice to advance health in each of these areas.

And finally, *body* will be herein defined as "the entire material or physical structure of a human being . . . the physical part of a person,"[3] originating from the Greek word *soma*. It is the perishable package unit that houses both the spirit and the three parts of a person's soul. It could be referred to as an earth suit, as it will perish in a person's finite time on this planet. The body health section of this book focuses on practical activities, exercises, and habits that will bring physical health and vibrancy to a person's body.

The body, mind, spirit order on the yoga sign is something we Americans inherited from ancient Greek philosophy, where the emphasis was on the body first. Many great things came out of the Greek emphasis on the physical—the beginning of the medical profession and the Olympics, being just a couple examples. But that order doesn't reflect God's order of spirit, soul, and body. The body is important, but it is only a temporary home for the spirit and soul.

While many in today's society focus solely on the body and neglect the spirit, many Christians do just the opposite, only focusing on spiritual growth. While spiritual development is vitally important and a large part of our calling as Christians, we do a disservice to ourselves when we neglect the soul and the body. No matter what background you're from, chances are you're ignoring proper soul care. In our current culture, there are very few people engaging in real conversations about the impact our feelings, thoughts, and actions have on our overall quality of life. In order to reach our highest potential in life, God leads us through 1 Thessalonians 5:23 to see how important it is to focus on all three parts—because all three are interconnected and vital to our overall well-being. We are essentially pneuma-psycho-somatic beings and we require focus on all three areas of our being in order to achieve the rhythm we need to flourish in life.

THE INTERCONNECTED PARTS

After my eureka moment, the visual analogy that came to mind was that of three interconnected tanks. The first tank is the spirit tank, which is filled when we focus on spiritual growth through activities such as prayer, Bible reading, and dreaming big about our purpose. The second tank is the soul tank, which is filled when we focus on developing health and wholeness in our minds, wills, and emotions. The third tank is the body, which is filled when we focus on proper nutrition, physical fitness, and rest.

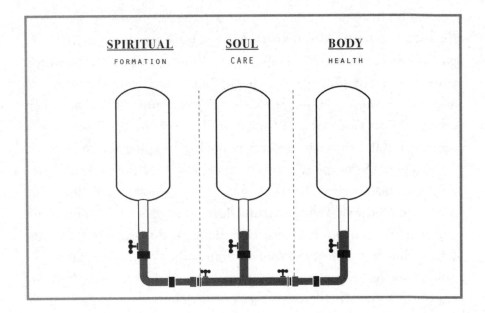

In this analogy, the three tanks are connected to each other with tubing. Caught up in my identity as a pastor, I spent the majority of my time filling my spirit tank. I was well-intentioned and could not afford to have the tank half full, so I focused on filling up that first tank all the way—to the neglect of the other two tanks. I did not consider my soul or my body as areas that were important to strengthen.

As I worked to fill up my spirit tank, I failed to recognize that the three tanks were interconnected. When one tank fills up while the others are essentially empty, simple physics comes into play. Since the tanks are interconnected, the level of the tank that is being filled simply decreases to the lowest common denominator in all three. The unfortunate truth I was learning was *if you overfocus on only one of your three areas, the one you focus on ends up leaking and not benefiting you to the proportion that you invest.* Take our spirits as an example. By overfocusing on spirit, you would think that you would grow by leaps and bounds based on your extreme focus. In actuality, you get very little growth based on your investment If you neglect your other two parts, your soul and your body. However, in contrast, by expending only a small amount of focus on all three areas of our lives—spirit, soul, and body—instead of just one, there is an instant and easy lift we receive in each area, something far greater than if we focus on only one. I had become a classic case study in a constant attempt to overfill my spirit tank without even realizing it. I was neglecting my soul and body, thinking that concentrating on my spirit alone would solve all of my burnout problems. It was an exercise in futility.

Remember that 1 Thessalonians 5:23 says, "The very God of peace sanctify you wholly; and I pray God your whole spirit and soul and body be preserved blameless unto the coming of our Lord Jesus Christ."[4] As the interconnected parts of our spirits, souls, and bodies each receives the attention it deserves, instead of being empty in one or more tanks, we will be whole: *complete in all respects.*

Based on this truth, once we find God's desired rhythm for our lives, spiritual fulfillment is going to be that much easier. Living a life in sync with God's rhythm and seeking to be complete in spiritual formation, soul care, and body health is actually more spiritual than just focusing on your spirit alone. In the following chapters, finding God's personal rhythm for you—not perfection in all areas—is the goal in building your whole life.

THE WHOLE LIFE WHEEL

A great self-assessment tool to see how balanced you are in your spirit, soul, and body is the Whole Life Wheel. The wheel represents a life that has rhythm, with all of its spokes tightened at the same pressure. When I was younger, I got into freestyle biking. (Yes, I am a product of the '80s, and freestyling was quite radical.) One key to a well-adjusted bike was to keep the spokes tightened: Bending and flexing on a bike with loose spokes could spell disaster. You need to focus on each spoke equally to create a strong, balanced life. I found concentrating on the weaker spokes on my Whole Life Wheel provided the quickest benefit to strengthening the whole of the wheel.

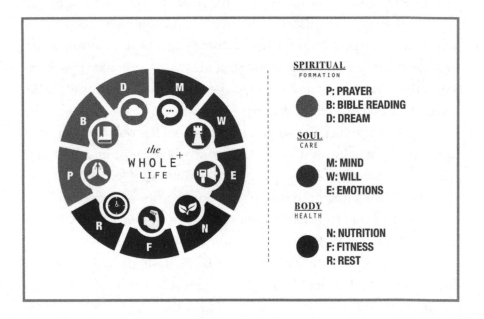

Spiritual Formation

The spiritual formation section of the Whole Life Wheel contains three basic components:

P stands for *Prayer.* Do you spend time each day in prayer? Are those prayers a quick fifteen-second "Help me God"– or "Please give me this"–type prayers? Or do you actually open your heart to Him and spend quality time with Him—and then allow Him the time and opportunity to speak to you?

B stands for *Bible reading.* How is your relationship to the written Word of God? Is your Bible sitting on your coffee table, gathering layers of dust? Is it an unused app on your phone or tablet? Or do you consistently spend time reading, meditating, and researching the wisdom of God?

D is for *Dream.* A dream is an understanding of the God-given trajectory and purpose of the path He has put you on in this season of life. Do you have a dream for the future that you believe He is calling you to accomplish?

Soul Care

The soul care section of the Whole Life Wheel includes your mind, will, and emotions.

M is for *Mind.* What does your thought life consist of? Is your mind a whirlpool of uncontrolled images and ideas? Or do you exercise control over your thought life, meditating on the good (see Philippians 4:8) and casting down every thought that you know is not from God (see 2 Corinthians 10:5)?

W reflects *Will.* Do you consistently choose to act according to God's plan for you? Or does your will follow the whims of your emotions and any people-pleasing tendencies to which you may be prone?

E stands for *Emotions.* Are you riding an emotional roller coaster every day (like I was in the introduction), up one moment and down the next, constantly moved by the circumstances of life? Or are your emotions settled and resting in the peace of God?

Body Health

The <u>body health</u> section of the Whole Life Wheel includes nutrition, fitness, and rest.

N focuses on *Nutrition.* A physical fitness expert told me that if I could do just one thing for my body, it should be eating right. She said that while working out is unarguably beneficial, good nutrition—eating nutritiously, hydrating frequently, taking needed supplements—is actually the most important component of body health. That is why the *N* section is the first of the three.

F stands for *Fitness*—your workout component. In our modern world of inactivity, it is essential for us to have a weekly plan—at least three times a week—to exercise the parts of our bodies that otherwise would not have their needed activity.

R for *Rest.* This last component is the one most often neglected. Rest definitely includes sleep, but we also focus on taking days off from work to play, reconnecting with those closest to you, and even taking extended break times every so often. Rest is a critical component to whole health.

HOW IS YOUR WHEEL ROLLING?

Are you ready to find out what your Whole Life Wheel looks like? So that you don't feel intimidated or discouraged before you even begin, let me be transparent and tell you what my wheel looked like at the time of my burnout. Because I had let two of my tanks run on empty for so long, my wheel was severely deflated and on the way to becoming totally flat! I was not moving down the road very fast. If my wheel had been attached to a car, I would have been the guy you pass on the interstate who has a completely deflated tire but keeps driving in hopes of making it to the next exit. With a wheel like that, it is hard for anyone to move forward in life with much success.

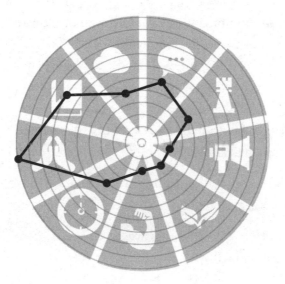

David Stine

The ultimate goal for all of us is to be healthy as possible so that we are prepared to face the circumstances that life brings with a confidence, a God confidence, that sets us up for victory.

Use the blank wheel below to rate each area of your life as it is today. Be honest and realistic. Fill in each segment of the wheel with a number between one and ten, with ten being the highest and furthest from the center of the wheel. A rating of one means that you are doing very poorly in that area of your life, a five means you are halfway to where you need to be, and a ten means you are doing great. You can use the following criteria to help you assess yourself in each area:

Spiritual Formation

+ *P = Prayer.* I have a vibrant prayer life and hear from God regularly.

+ *B = Bible reading.* I am regularly reading and applying God's Word to my life.

+ *D = Dream.* I understand and am walking toward God's purpose for this season of my life.

Soul Care

+ *M = Mind.* My thoughts about God, myself, and others line up with Scripture.

+ *W = Will.* My will is in line with what I believe God's priorities are for my life.

+ *E = Emotion.* My emotions are healthy and submitted to my mind and will.

Body Health

+ *N = Nutrition.* I am eating nutritiously, hydrating frequently, and taking any needed supplements.

+ *F = Fitness.* I am in good physical health and exercising at least three times a week.

✦ **R = Rest.** I am creating space in my life for daily, weekly, and quarterly rest.

Congratulations on filling out your Whole Life Wheel! Hopefully you now see more clearly the areas you need to work on as you journey to wholeness.

LIVING THE WHOLE LIFE TODAY

Since understanding this Whole Life revelation, living in God's rhythm is becoming a natural way of life. I am still a work in progress and certainly don't live out all the steps perfectly, but I am more intentional and regularly check in with myself to gauge how I am doing in each area by filling out my own Whole Life Wheel.

What about you? After evaluating your wheel and determining what areas need attention, are you ready to take the next steps toward your whole life? I know that change is hard, and rearranging or adding to your daily obligations may seem overwhelming, but the overall goal is to *find the best personal rhythm for you* so it becomes an enjoyable part of your lifestyle.

It is important to remember that your current commitments, your individual circumstances, and the condition of each area affects how much capacity you have to work on your wheel at present, which is normal and understandable. It is also important to note that God will lead you to focus on some areas more intentionally, depending on your season in life, so your wheel may not look perfectly round at all times. What is most important is that you are listening to God and asking Him what areas to focus on now and how you can partner with Him to grow toward greater wholeness in whatever season you're in. I've found in many seasons since my Whole Life journey has begun that He opens opportunities to work on areas that I would not have otherwise considered.

After studying 1 Thessalonians 5:23 and committing to implementing its truths into our lives, it is imperative we look at the next verse. First Thessalonians 5:24 says, "The one who calls you is faithful, and *he will do it*" (emphasis mine).

This truth is a powerful reminder of the partnership He invites anyone to share with Him. There is freedom in knowing that creating a Whole Life rhythm doesn't just depend on you. Yes, you must acknowledge which tank is empty or that your wheel is flat. Then, based on what you discover, you must decide to change and commit to the process we'll lay out in the chapters to follow. As you do so, God will be right beside you to help! Finding your Whole Life rhythm is His heart for you. You are not alone in this process, and as much as you want to succeed in experiencing a whole life, He wants you to succeed even more.

I am excited for the journey you are embarking upon, because as you follow the principles shared in this book, I believe that your life, like mine, will be transformed beyond imagination.

REVIEW

In this first chapter I introduced the revelation that I received from 1 Thessalonians 5:23 that you and I are composed of three parts: a spirit which gives us God consciousness; a soul which gives us self-consciousness; and a body. We saw through the diagram of the tanks that all three parts are interconnected and have a profound influence on each other. When we neglect one or more of the tanks, it affects the others.

In this chapter I also introduced the Whole Life Wheel and its three sections of spiritual formation, soul care, and body health. For each of the three sections there are three areas that affect the health of that section: *Spiritual Formation* = prayer, Bible reading, and dream; *Soul Care* = mind, will, and emotion; and *Body Health* = nutrition, fitness, and rest.

WHOLE LIFE CHALLENGE

At the end of each chapter there will be a challenge for you to complete. For this chapter's challenge, I suggest finding a Whole Life partner or partners: a person or a small group who will commit to going through this book with you. The mutual support of an individual or group will keep you, and them, accountable to the challenges presented throughout this book.

Your Whole Life partner will be your number one encourager as you work to bring balance and wholeness to the nine areas listed on the Whole Life Wheel. Choose a person or persons who are living a God-first life that you feel comfortable sharing openly with—someone who can make the time each week to check in with you. You might just find that their life is changing in addition to yours and be able to encourage them as you start this journey to wholeness.

part one

Spiritual Formation

IN THE BEGINNING OF RECORDED HISTORY, the Old Testament tells us that God created man, forming him from dust and breathing into his nostrils the breath of life. God created a physical body from the earth and then breathed His Spirit into it. The Spirit gave life to the body and man became a living soul. From that point forward, humans have had a spiritual nature and a soul within a physical body.[1]

In the New Testament, Ephesians 2:4–5 explains that before we came to Christ, we were spiritually dead. When we accept Christ into our lives, God sends His Holy Spirit to live inside of us. Our spirits become fully alive and cleansed. Our spirits are perfected at the moment of salvation, but we have to be intentional to stay connected to God and allow His Spirit to lead our spirits. It's through our human spirit that we have communion and fellowship with God, and our intuition, the ability to determine right from wrong, is derived from our spirits.[2]

In this section, we will focus on what fills our spirit tanks, what feeds our spiritual growth, and how we can position ourselves for a greater and stronger connection to God. In Dallas Willard's article "Spiritual Formation: What It Is, and How It Is Done," he defines spiritual formation as "the process of transformation of the inmost dimension of the human being . . . It is being formed (really, transformed) in such a way that its natural expression comes to be the deeds of Christ done in the power of Christ."[3]

Spiritual formation is not limited to the spirit, but it *begins* there. If spiritual formation is the transformation of our innermost being to become more like Christ, as Willard explains, then the transformation of the spirit will lead to transformation in our whole beings as our spirits influence and lead our souls and bodies.

There are three foundational disciplines that are necessary to fill our spirit tanks. The first chapter in this section is on prayer: connecting with God and developing a vibrant prayer life.

The second chapter in this section focuses on the Bible as a source of spiritual food, direction in life, and power.

The final chapter in this section is about God's dream for your life. Each season of your life has amazing purpose in it, and I will give you some ideas on how to discover and walk toward your own God-sized dream.

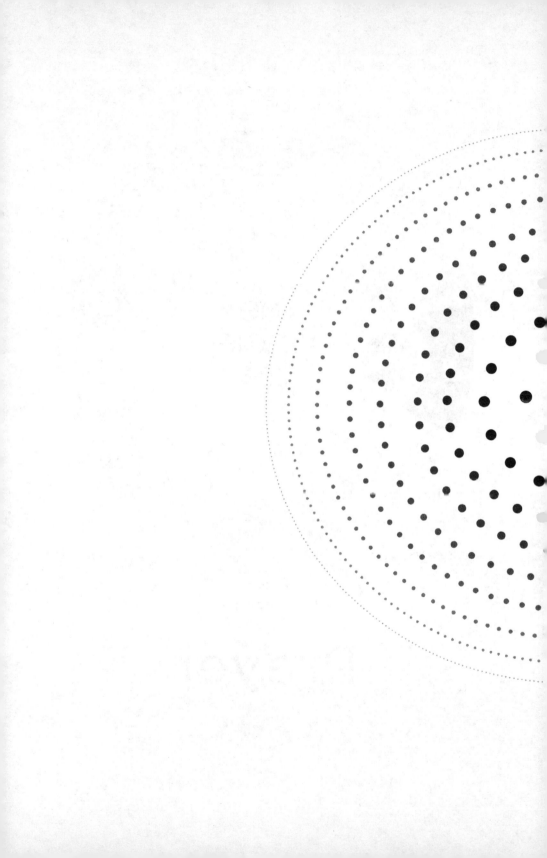

the
whole
life

Prayer

two

Prayer—The Secret to a Powerful Life

Prayer is not asking.
Prayer is putting oneself in the hands of God, at His disposition,
and listening to His voice in the depth of our Hearts.
—Mother Teresa

Lord, teach us to pray . . .
—The Disciples, Luke 11:1

Out of all the things the disciples could have asked Jesus to teach them, they had one primary request: They wanted to pray like Jesus. Luke 11:1 says, "One day Jesus was praying in a certain place. When he finished, one of his disciples said to him, 'Lord, teach us to pray, just as John taught his disciples.'"

In Luke 11, a majority of Jesus' ministry had already occurred. The disciples had been following Jesus for almost three years. They had seen Him do amazing signs, wonders, and miracles—yet, at the end of this particular day, it's hard to believe that the only thing they asked Jesus to teach them was to pray.

If I had been one of the disciples, I doubt that the thing I would have asked Jesus for is how to pray. I would have first said, "Jesus, teach me how to walk on water!" so I could drive all my friends down the road from my home to the ocean and show them what Jesus had taught me. I might or might not have also asked Jesus to teach me how to perform miracles, if for no other reason than to cut down on my family of six's medical bills. But no, the disciples simply asked the Lord to teach them how to pray.

I think that, after a few years of traveling with Jesus, they finally began to realize that each time He finished another amazing period of ministry—healing people, casting out demons, raising the dead, multiplying food—He consistently slipped away to a secluded place to communicate with His Father. I am sure that they began to recognize that all the power Jesus displayed in His ministry was directly connected to one thing: *prayer*. And if they wanted to be effective in ministry, they needed to tap into the same source of Jesus' power. Like them, I distinctly remember the first time I realized the secret connection between power and prayer in my father's life.

A GOOD FATHER

I have a good dad who has been very successful in life; it seems like everything he puts his hand to prospers. He was a U.S. Air Force officer who was promoted many times and won numerous awards for his service. He was an entrepreneur, expanding the family business with his brothers, opening numerous locations of their home improvement store throughout Louisiana and into Mississippi. His favorite hobby was sailing, and he won many of the regattas he entered. He was respected as a man of integrity and well-loved in our small town of Lake Charles, Louisiana—but by no one more than me. My dad is my hero. As a young boy, I wondered at his secret to power and success in life.

My dad was the strong, silent type when it came to talking about his faith. He held the philosophy that your life should speak louder than your words, much like Francis of Assisi who is claimed to have said, "Preach the gospel at all times, and if you have to, use words."[1] He never missed a church service (unfortunately, much to my dismay as a teenager, neither did I) and he served in several leadership roles in our local church community.

He is also a man of private prayer. When I was about eight years old, I noticed something about my dad's daily routine that, at the time, I thought was odd. In the morning my dad got on his knees right beside his bed, folded his hands, and bowed his head in prayer. I noticed that he did it every day, not just some days. I also noticed that he actually did the same thing every night. I wondered why he did this: What did he gain from this practice?

As a teenager, I wandered into my parents' bedroom one day and went to my dad's side of the bed. Sure enough, there were two worn spots in the carpet where his knees touched every morning and every night. It was then that I recognized there was a direct correlation between prayer and the man of character I knew my dad to be, as well as the favor he experienced. It became abundantly clear to me that there was *power* in prayer.

My dad's prayer life made a huge impression on me and made me want to become a man of prayer myself. My dad never told me to pray; he simply modeled prayer. The disciples had the same realization watching Jesus' life and figured out that, of everything they could ask Jesus to teach them, it should be prayer.

Maybe you are new to prayer but want to know more. Perhaps you believe in the power of prayer, but your prayer life is primarily shooting up quick requests when you are driving to work or at random points during your day as needs arise. Or maybe, like my dad, you have been walking with God for years and have a consistent prayer life. However you ranked your prayer life on the Whole Life Wheel, you can enhance your relationship with God and take it to a deeper, more personal level as you invest in more intentional, focused prayer. The incredible thing about growing in God is we can never reach a plateau so high that we're finished with our spiritual growth in this life. He is so immense that there's always more of Him that we can experience. God is always inviting us to more, but we have to first accept this invitation and take the next step to meet Him where He is and with the method He gave us . . . prayer.

BUSTING MYTHS ABOUT PRAYER

Before we jump into how to practically grow your prayer life, I want to bust some common myths about prayer. My boys—Isaac, Josiah, and Asher—used to love watching the show *MythBusters*—the long-running Discovery Channel series. Two Hollywood special effects experts attempted to debunk urban legends and myths by directly testing them with cool gadgets and lots of explosives. By the end of each episode, each myth was rated "busted," "plausible," or "confirmed." I know the show is a little dated now, but everyone loves a good myth on the chopping block, so I want to give you a few myths about prayer that need to be busted.

MYTH #1—Prayer is boring.

Before I realized the power of prayer in my dad's life, I felt quite indifferent toward prayer. It always seemed like a one-way conversation. When I prayed, I asked God to bless everyone in my family and to help me with whatever activities or tests I had coming up. Then I was done. I could easily finish in one minute flat—maybe one minute and fifteen seconds if I knew someone who was sick. I was baffled by the idea of spending an hour in prayer and wondered what the heck those people talked about for that long.

My reality was that God felt very distant to me. I heard my grandparents talk about hearing from God, but that concept was so foreign to me that I thought it was reserved for the super-spiritual. Prayer felt like a religious duty where I piously presented formulated requests to what felt like a very stoic God. I often wondered if there was more. It felt as though I had to read or memorize the same prayers and read them over and over and over again. It didn't seem enjoyable at all.

MYTH #1 BUSTED! THE TRUTH: Prayer is an invitation to an ever-unfolding adventure.

After I surrendered my life to God and began to grow in my faith, I realized that prayer was a means by which to know God personally. I was taught that I could, in plain conversation, be raw and real with God about whatever was on my mind. If I listened, He would speak back to me. It has definitely been a process of much trial and error to learn to recognize His voice, but it has transformed my prayer life from a monotonous, sterile routine into an exciting adventure and active, two-way conversation with the living God.

I realized that prayer is not boring because God isn't boring. He is the most interesting, fascinating being that has ever existed, and He invites each of us to know Him and the power we have through Him. In *The Pursuit of God*, A. W. Tozer explains that not all believers have come to this realization. "For millions of Christians . . . God is no more real than He is to the non-Christian. They go through life trying to love an ideal and be loyal to a mere principle."[2] He goes on to clarify that God actually really wants to be known but we have to accept the invitation: "Over against all this cloudy vagueness stands the clear scriptural doctrine that *God can be known in personal experience*. A loving Personality dominates the Bible, walking among the trees of the garden and breathing fragrance over every scene. Always a living Person is present, speaking, pleading, loving, working, and manifesting Himself whenever and wherever His people have the receptivity necessary to receive the manifestation" (emphasis mine).[3]

MYTH #2—Prayer is only for emergencies.

Sometimes we treat prayer like that end-of-the-game Hail Mary pass. When we get in desperate situations, we think, *I am not sure what else to do, and it certainly doesn't hurt to pray, so I guess I'll throw one upstairs to see if anything happens.* Examples of "prayer triage" include praying for a passing grade on a test you didn't study for or favor with your boss when you oversleep and show up an hour late for work. If you've ever done that, don't worry—I used to approach prayer the same way. After my emergency passed, I wouldn't pray again until the next desperate situation arose.

MYTH #2 BUSTED! THE TRUTH: Prayer is an invitation to consistent communication with God.

Prayer is all about developing an authentic, ongoing relationship with God. It is a place of honesty, interaction, giving and receiving, speaking and listening. God is not a formula, a vending machine, or a cosmic Santa Claus. He does not want to simply be turned to in times of need or when we want Him to give us something. In Isaiah 43:5, God says, "I am with you."

I first learned this powerful reality—that I can enjoy His presence and conversation wherever I go—when I lived in a fourteen-by-eight-foot trailer in DeRidder, Louisiana. (That was definitely way before the tiny house trend!) I felt extremely humbled living there, and if I am honest, I had a bad attitude about it; I hated it.

I moved there, taking a 75 percent pay cut after working at a large department store headquarters, to start my first full-time ministry job leading a youth group. That was a lonely season for me, as I lived in an extremely small town with almost no one else my age. My trailer was in the middle of a cow pasture, and cows would rub themselves along the sides of it at all hours of the night. I couldn't believe that was my reality. I honestly felt like I was at the end of my rope, but I loved the church and really loved that group of kids in the youth group.

I knew conceptually that God was with me in that season, but I had a hard time picturing Him in the room—that is, until the day He met me at Popeyes fast-food restaurant. I would save up my money and drive through Popeyes as a special treat to get a three-piece spicy dark chicken meal with red beans, rice, and a biscuit. One afternoon when I was feeling a little desolate, I took a trip to Popeyes, but when

I pulled up to the drive-through to order, I found myself ordering not one but two three-piece spicy chicken meals. I drove home and set the table for two—and spent the next hour in His presence over lunch, talking to Him across the table about all that was on my heart. Many people have asked me through the years of telling this story, what did I do with that extra lunch when I was finished talking to God? Each time I tell them that I ended up eating his lunch too; after all, God would surely not want it to go to waste, right?

I was in a season of practicing communing with God. I remember distinctly reading a book called *The Practice of the Presence of God*[4] by Brother Lawrence, a seventeenth-century monk who visualized God standing in front of Him as he tended to his assigned task of washing the dishes. Following Brother Lawrence's lead helped me to visualize God sitting across from me over lunch and has made a way for me to see Him sitting across from me in empty chairs today.

God wants an open line of communication for you to talk with Him whenever you want. I like to think of it kind of like this: During the Cold War, Russia made an agreement with Havana to put missiles in Cuba. Our intelligence services discovered what was happening, which led to a week and a half of complete panic in the United States. Experts say it was the closest that we have ever come to World War III. About ten days into the crisis, President John F. Kennedy contacted the Russian premier, Nikita Khrushchev, and told him they could not have missiles in Cuba. Khrushchev, faced with this ultimatum, eventually backed down and had the missiles removed and the crisis was over.

One positive thing that emerged from that crisis was that Russia and the United States decided they were going to set up a clear, uninhibited, direct line of communication between the two countries. In pop culture, this is symbolized by the ubiquitous red phone. It represented that there was direct and clear communication between the two nations' leaders, without relying on an operator or middleman. They didn't even have to dial; they could just pick up the phone and talk to the other side anytime, twenty-four hours a day, seven days a week, 365 days a year. *This is what God offers to each of us.* For many years I kept a red phone on my desk to remind me to never take this profound reality for granted. People often asked me about my red phone when they came to my office. I always told them the same thing, "It's my direct line." It served as a constant physical reminder to talk to God when I couldn't seem to figure something out or when I simply needed someone to talk to.

MYTH #3—Prayer is ineffective.

Another common myth about prayer is that our prayers don't really make a difference. I have definitely wrestled with this, wondering if prayer is just an exercise in futility. Have you ever felt like your prayers were just bouncing off the ceiling? Or maybe you believe it is an effective exercise for others but have struggled to believe it would really work for you. Or perhaps you have wondered why some prayers get answered and others do not—at least, not in the time frame or way you requested.

I've experienced seasons where receiving the desired answers to my prayers was hit-or-miss, with much more emphasis on the miss. On those occasions when my prayers were answered, I wondered if that would have happened regardless of whether or not I prayed. I was sure I was doing something wrong, but I didn't know what.

MYTH #3 BUSTED! THE TRUTH: Prayer is an invitation to partner with God.

Through the testimony of many believers throughout history, we know prayer changes circumstances. In the process of seeing God move in our own situations, we are changed. There is still much mystery surrounding exactly how prayer works, but I have no doubt that when we pray, God not only listens but moves on our behalf.

In Matthew 6:9–10, Jesus prayed, "Our Father in heaven, hallowed be your name, your kingdom come, your will be done, *on earth as it is in heaven*" (emphasis mine). When we pray this way, we are asking for the dominion of God's Kingdom to be done here in our midst on earth today. Bill Johnson, a favorite author of mine, said, "What is free to operate in Heaven—joy, peace, wisdom, health, wholeness, and all the other good promises we read about in the Bible—should be free to operate here on this planet, in your home, your church, your business, and your school. What is not free to operate there—sickness, disease, spiritual bondage, and sin should not be free to operate here, period."[5] Our role as believers is to help bring the realities of heaven to earth through prayer. The real reward of prayer isn't simply receiving the answer—although I like that part, too—but entering into a place of partnership with God to bring His will here on this earth.

God is inviting you into this dynamic partnership of knowing Him and walking with Him. In Jeremiah 9:23–24, God instructs His people, "Let not a wise man boast of his wisdom, and let not the mighty man boast of his might, let not a rich man boast of his riches; but let him who boasts boast of this, that he understands and knows Me, that I am the Lord who exercises lovingkindness, justice and righteousness on earth; for I delight in these things" (NASB). If there is anything that we are going to boast about, God says that it should be that we know and understand Him.

WHEN AND WHERE TO PRAY

Now that I've busted some common myths about prayer, I hope you understand that prayer is an invitation to an unfolding adventure of communication and partnership with God. It is a catalyst to know Him on a much deeper level. I believe wherever you are in your spiritual formation, God wants you to know Him more fully and lead you into a consistent and dynamic prayer life.

A couple years ago, I was invited along with some other D.C.-area pastors to meet the president of the United States. The day of the meeting, I woke up with the awareness that I was going to meet with our nation's leader. My thought process was different that day as I prepared myself mentally and physically and rehearsed what I would say to him when I got my personal, face-to-face moment in his presence.

Entering through White House security, hoping my Social Security number checked out, waiting for an additional two hours prior to the actual meeting, and wondering about the delays, I was acutely aware of what all the preparation and process was leading to: a moment with the most powerful man in the world. Similarly, when I spend time with God, I am about to meet with the ruler of the known and unknown universe. My prayers, worship, Bible study, and journaling are for one purpose: to meet with Him. If my goal the day I met the president was to optimize my moment with him, how much more should I optimize my daily moments with God?

The time and place I meet with God has changed through the years. When I was a bachelor, I had a futon that became my place of prayer; later it was a special chair where I sat when I would spend time with Him. I also had a season when I would walk around the neighborhood focusing on Him and His presence.

The most important thing is getting consistent about prayer, so if you can't find a "special" place to pray, just identify a period in your daily routine where you have some free time. You can pray anywhere: on the subway, in the bathroom as you get ready in the morning, or in the carpool lane. As I'm writing this book, my time to meet with Him is first thing in the morning after my workout, before my day gets crowded with appointments and family commitments. I meet with Him after my workout because any earlier I'd be half-asleep—not optimal to spend quality time with Him.

My current place to meet with Him is at the coffee shop across the street from the Y. I try to sit in the same spot and order the same drink, tea, every day. With an empty chair in front of me to symbolize His presence, I pop in my earbuds and use a playlist of calming worship music on my phone to focus my attention.

As a stay-at-home mom, my wife, Taryn, has been creative in finding her time and place to meet with God, based on the season in our children's lives. When all the kids were home, she rose thirty minutes before the rest of the family, or stayed up at night after the kids were in bed and settled in a chair in the living room. When the kids started school, after dropping them off, she went to her favorite coffee shop. In each of the different times and places her routine was the same: listening to worship music, Bible readying and study, prayer, and journaling.

Recently I did a study of some Hebrew words with a fellow pastor friend who is an expert in the Hebrew language and ancient Jewish culture. We learned that the Jewish people through the time of Jesus would not have necessarily prayed in a loud voice. The Jews believed that the Kingdom of God is not a place that is far off in the clouds but right here with us. The Greek word *pneuma*, which is usually translated as spirit, or breath, can also be translated as atmosphere. The Jews believed that God is the literal atmosphere around us, everywhere, all the time, and our every breath is in Him. Sometimes they'd put their knees against their chests and wrap their prayer shawls around their bodies, letting the shawl hang three to six inches in front of their eyes. When a Jew did this, he would sit in quiet devotion while focusing on God's Spirit in the atmosphere—that space between his face and the shawl, his breath—recognizing the closeness and intimacy of the Lord in his time of devotion.

John Wesley, who became the founder of the Methodist movement and one of the best-known Anglican ministers of the 1700s, had a mother who understood the importance of doing whatever it took to spend time alone with God. Living in poverty with her nineteen children and an often absent husband, she did not have the luxury of getting out of the house to have uninterrupted devotional times with

God. But she did have an apron. When she wanted to shut out the world around her and focus on His presence in prayer, she covered her head with her apron. The children all knew not to bother their mother when the apron was covering her because she was spending time with God.

Your place and time with God may not be the same as mine, but I encourage you to carve out times when you are at your best—mentally alert and physically rested—and find your special place to meet with Him. The location and time will become sacred space, as you will have the expectation that you are going to meet with God.

HOW TO PRAY

As you find your time and place to meet with God, there are a few different ways you can direct your prayer. I focus my time with Him on praying, reading Scripture, and journaling what I believe His Spirit is saying to me.

A commonly known acronym, ACTS, can help you intentionally integrate different foundational components of prayer into your time with God. ACTS stands for Adoration, Confession, Thanksgiving, and Supplication. You can spend just a few minutes on each area and then move on to the next area as you feel led. (Please note that you may not want to do this type of prayer in a coffee shop unless you are writing in a journal.)

1. Adoration

Start your prayer saying what you appreciate about God. Psalm 117 models this: "Praise the Lord, all you nations. Praise Him, all you people of the earth. For His unfailing love for us is powerful; the Lord's faithfulness endures forever" (NLT). When we begin our prayers with adoration, we are reminded how amazing God is and how worthy He is of our worship. Sometimes we need to remind ourselves of how small our problems are compared to how big God is, and beginning with a time of worship and adoration does this. What do you love most about God? What qualities have you especially appreciated about Him recently?

2. Confession

Next, share anything that you need to ask His forgiveness for or confess to Him. *Sin* is an archery term that means to miss the mark. If there is any area where you know you have missed the mark, either intentionally or unintentionally, seek and receive His forgiveness. David models this in Psalm 51:1–2, "Have mercy on me, O God, because of your unfailing love. Because of your great compassion, blot out the stain of my sins. Wash me clean from my guilt. Purify me from my sin."[6]

3. Thanksgiving

What are you thankful for? You can thank God for what He has done in your life or for your family, friends, and circumstances. You can thank Him for His faithfulness to you or how He has worked all things together for good in your life. Psalm 118:1 reminds us of the importance of thanking God for His goodness to us, "Give thanks to the Lord, for He is good; his love endures forever."

4. Supplication

Supplication, very simply, is asking for things. You can ask for personal needs or the needs of others. James 4:2 says, "You do not have because you do not ask God." It took me years to fully understand and articulate this principle in my heart. God is not motivated by your need but by you asking Him to meet your need. We serve a God who desires to be close to us and in a relationship with us.

You can ask God to meet physical needs, but you can also remind God of the promises in His Word and ask Him to move in areas so that His promises become a reality in those circumstances. Hebrews 4:16 encourages us to boldly approach God with our supplication: "Let us then approach God's throne of grace with confidence, so that we may receive mercy and find grace to help us in our time of need." Charles Spurgeon said, "God never shuts His storehouses of blessings until you shut your mouth."[7] You must ask God!

I am often asked what to do after you have prayed over an area in your life and are anxiously awaiting the answer. You can be real with God about how you are feeling, but know that He does not intend for you to stay in a place of anxiety. Philippians 4:6–7 says, "Do not be anxious about anything, but in every situation, by prayer and petition, with thanksgiving, present your requests to God. And the peace of God, which transcends all understanding, will guard your hearts and your minds in Christ Jesus."

It does not matter what the issue is: Worrying about something going on in life—a relational issue, your finances, something at work, or even World War III—is not productive! Jesus said not to be anxious about *anything* because He has a plan, and that plan is for your highest good. He also says to bring your concerns to Him and to *leave* them with Him. When I give my wife a present, she expects me to leave it with her. (This is why, if I buy her something I want, I have learned to buy myself one, too!) After you present and leave your requests and concerns, He in turn lets you know if you've fully released your anxiety.

When you have fully yielded to God your grip on the situation, you will have a deep and abiding peace within you. Whenever I pray, I anticipate receiving that peace, even when I don't understand how God's going to fix the problem. That peace is His promise to us, and He never fails to keep His promises.

OTHER METHODS OF PRAYER

The last thing I want for your prayer life is for it to seem formulaic, so I encourage you rotating the ACTS method with some of the following methods. Use the one that fits you most naturally. If you are seasoned in the area of prayer, try one that you haven't used a lot in the past.

Intercession

Similar to supplication, intercession is generally focused on praying for others. James 5:16 says, "The prayer of a righteous person is powerful and effective." As we understand the authority we have as believers, we realize the importance of our call to intercession: As our weak words come into agreement with God's heart, circumstances around us literally shift. Jesus is the ultimate intercessor. 1 Timothy 2:5–6 explains, "For there is one God and one mediator between God and mankind, the man Christ Jesus, who gave himself as a ransom for all people."

Contemplating this concept recently, I realized intercession is not merely praying but the act of bringing together the two sides. Jesus brought us together with the Father. When we intercede, we have the honor of bringing people together with the Father, figuratively holding on to them and holding on to the Father and interceding for an intersection of His will with theirs. When I see intercession through this lens, it gets me even more excited to contend in prayer on behalf of those God has placed in my life.

In the movie *War Room*, Elizabeth and her husband Tony seem to have it all, but underneath the veneer there is an eroding marriage, verbal abuse, and the emotional neglect of their little girl, who just wants the love and affection of her absentee father. Elizabeth is a real estate agent, who has a wise, elderly client named Miss Clara. Miss Clara shows Elizabeth a special closet she has dedicated to praying, and calls it her war room because she explains, "In order to stand up and fight the enemy, you need to get on your knees and pray." Miss Clara challenges Elizabeth to intercede for her husband and for their marriage to be restored. As Elizabeth starts to contend for her husband in her war room (aka her walk-in closet), things begin to shift. Elizabeth fights for her marriage from a place of prayer, and, as a result, her husband's heart eventually turns back toward God, Elizabeth, and their daughter.

Your war room doesn't need to be a physical closet like Elizabeth's, but we all need to find a place of intercession where we can partner with God in prayer. As we petition for God's Kingdom to come into whatever relationship or situation we are praying for, we will see circumstances shift as we come into divine alignment with our Creator. We see this concept of intercession taught in Ezekiel 22:30 where God is looking for someone to stand in the gap before Him on behalf of the land—so He would not have to destroy the land.

I recommend that you create a list of areas in which God is calling you to intercede. Psalm 144:1 says, "Praise be to the Lord my Rock, who trains my hands for war, my fingers for battle." One way I have heard children's ministers teach children to pray is to remember the areas you want to pray about by assigning different topics to different fingers. This simplifies remembering your prayer list because you always have it with you and it trains your fingers for the most important type of battle.

Your thumb can represent those closest to you: your family and friends. You can lift up any needs they have or anything you are asking God to make happen in their lives. Your pointer finger can be for those who point you in the right direction, such as teachers, mentors, and pastors. (We pastors love your prayers!) Your middle finger is the tallest, so this can represent those who lead you, such as governmental leaders, to have wisdom and discernment. The ring finger is your weakest finger, so it can represent those who are sick or in need; Scripture teaches these people are close to God's heart. The pinkie is the smallest, so it can be a reminder to pray for either your own needs or anything or anybody else on your heart.

I am often asked what to do with prayers that do not get answered the way I would like or do not happen according to the timing I was hoping for. I have found that, even in times of doubt, the most important thing is to trust in the One who answers and focus on His goodness. If this is the lens through which I see all circumstances, even when the circumstances are not what I prefer, I won't wrongly assess His character because He did not answer the prayer in the way I wanted. I stand upon the promise in Romans 8:28, which says He works all things together for our good.

Prophetic Prayer

Prophecy is a fancy word for hearing from God and sharing what you hear, so prophetic prayer for others is simply praying for someone and sharing what you believe God, through the Holy Spirit, is saying. Prophecy is one of the spiritual gifts listed in 1 Corinthians 12:10 and Romans 12:6. While some may have a more developed gift in this area, I believe this is a gift God gives to all believers. First Corinthians 14:1 encourages all believers to desire the gifts of the spirit, especially prophecy.

First Corinthians 14:3 tells us the purpose of prophecy is to strengthen, encourage, and comfort others. When I pray for someone else, I ask God to give me something specific that will strengthen, encourage, and comfort them. If this type of prayer is new to you, I challenge you to try it. You could start by asking God to give you a word for your Whole Life partner, a close friend, or family member.

Sometimes this word comes in the form of a Bible verse, an idea, or even a picture in your mind's eye. I encourage you to close your eyes and ask God, "What do you want to say to my Whole Life partner, friend, family member, or spouse?" Pay close attention to your thoughts. Does a Bible verse come to mind? This could either be a reference like Genesis 1:1, "In the beginning . . ." or you could remember the content of a verse. Google or Siri comes in very handy: "What is the Bible verse that says, 'In the beginning . . .'?"

Does a thought or phrase come to your mind when you pray for him or her? Maybe it is something simple like *Step out.* You don't have to understand the full meaning or implications of the word; you simply need to deliver what you are sensing. Maybe there is an area God is calling your Whole Life partner, family member, or friend to step out in and He will use your encouragement as confirmation. Maybe you see a picture of an object or a scene. You can ask God what this picture means, if there is any interpretation you are supposed to share, or if you are to just share what you saw. If you are not sure if the thought is from you or God, I encourage you just to share it and ask them to pray that God will confirm if it is from Him.

Proverbs 25:11 says, "Like golden apples set in silver is a word spoken at the right time" (ISV). As you pray for someone, I believe God loves to give you just the right word at just the right time to give strength to others.

Fast and Pray

Although not my favorite spiritual discipline, I have seen incredible results from times of prayer and fasting: denying yourself food and drink for the purpose of spending that time in prayer. I have even grown to love fasting in certain repects. The rewards of fasting include stronger awareness of God's presence, greater alertness to spiritual matters, breakthroughs in stagnant or ongoing difficult circumstances, and increased spiritual power in prayer. The greatest benefit is connecting more deeply with Him. I have personally experienced some of my most significant encounters with God during these times. I have always said, "Victory comes fast to those who fast." I recommend spending the time that you normally spend preparing and eating food in prayer and studying God's Word, so that you intentionally position yourself to meet with Him. Some of the more common types of fasts include:

+ **Specific Fast**—You abstain from certain food(s) or drink(s) that are especially enticing to you.

+ **Partial Fast**—You fast one meal a day for one or more days a week.

+ **Daniel Fast**—You abstain from meat, sugar, dairy, alcohol, and processed foods. Instead you eat fruits, vegetables, whole grains, and nuts. This fast is modeled after Daniel 10:2–3.

+ **Liquid Fast**—You abstain from food and only drink juices and other liquids.

+ **Water Fast**—You abstain from food and liquids other than water. This is generally best for shorter periods of time if you are not an experienced faster.

+ **Media Fast**—Typically, biblical fasting means refraining from food for spiritual purposes, but some also choose to fast from different forms of media and entertainment, such as movies, social media, television, or the Internet, to remove distractions and have more time for prayer and for investing in their relationship with God.

To clarify, fasting without prayer is called starvation. The idea of denying oneself food or some activity with the intent of drawing closer to God requires prayer. Even though fasting can be one of the more challenging spiritual disciplines to our flesh, it is ultimately an incredible gift from God designed to lead us into a place of greater freedom. Richard Foster, author of *Celebration of Discipline: The Path to Spiritual Growth*,[8] observes that fasting, more than any other discipline, reveals areas of our lives that have a propensity to be idols.

When the comfort of food is stripped away, we often run to other places such as entertainment, shopping, or other forms of escapism for pleasure rather than first running to God to satisfy our hearts. He is trying to teach us to "feast on the abundance of your house . . . give them drink from your river of delights" (Psalm 36:8). Fasting and prayer is an invitation to place Him first in our lives again and to experience greater intimacy with Him.

Many of the heroes of the Bible modeled a lifestyle of fasting and prayer: Moses, Hannah, Samuel, David, Esther, Elijah, John the Baptist, Anna, Jesus, Paul, and the disciples. Throughout Scripture you can read stories of men and women who humbled themselves before God through fasting and prayer and experienced God moving dramatically in their lives.

You don't need to be a spiritual giant to fast and pray. In fact, fasting was considered a normal part of a believer's life in both the Old Testament and the New Testament. In Matthew 6:16, Jesus told his disciples, "When you fast . . ." Notice he did not say, "If you fast . . ." I encourage you to pray that God will show you what He wants you to lay down for a fast as an expression of worship to Him. I believe as you place yourself in a position of voluntary weakness and set a time to draw closer to Him, He will show up in a significant way.

If you have health issues or concerns, or are currently on medication, please consult your doctor before going without food for multiple days.

Inquiring of God

One of the easiest and most natural types of prayer to integrate into your life is something the Bible calls "inquiring of the Lord." This is simply asking God questions. We see this modeled throughout Scripture, but nowhere is it highlighted more than in David's life. Before David went into battle, he "inquired of God," asking if he should move forward. There are eleven battles recorded in the books of 1 and 2

Samuel. Every time David entered into one of those battles, before the Jews suited up or even met to figure out the battle plan, it says David did the same thing: "He inquired of the Lord." One of those battles is found in 2 Samuel 5:2, where the Philistines were attacking the people of God with the goals of devastating David and his men and proving that their gods were stronger than the God of Israel.

David's response in the face of the threat was to inquire of the Lord. He faced a great challenge, so he went to God in prayer for direction and help. After asking God if he should attack the Philistines, 2 Samuel 5:23 says that "He answered." David inquired of the Lord, and *God answered back*. That wasn't just a one-way call. There was actually somebody on the other end giving David some instruction. David did what the Lord commanded and defeated the Philistines.

The concept of inquiring of the Lord should not be reserved just for major life decisions or for Old Testament saints. God wants to be "inquired of" in our day-to-day lives. I personally inquire of the Lord throughout my day over matters that may seem small to some, but I desire His wisdom and leadership in all things. When I am in a difficult meeting, I ask God to help me discern the root of the difficulty and inquire of Him if there's a question I should ask that will get to the root of the problem. When I feel overwhelmed by my task list, I take a moment to ask God for His wisdom with regard to what to tackle first and what strategies He wants me to implement in order to accomplish all that He would have me do that day. Here is a basic example of this type of prayer:

God, I ask that You would help me with this huge list of things I have to do today. It's a particularly long list, but I know with Your help I can get all these things done quickly and hassle-free. I give You my day and ask that I would see Your hand working many times today. Thank You so much for helping me, in Jesus' name. Amen!

I even inquire of God when I need some date ideas for me and Taryn or activities to do with my children. I simply ask, "What activity would bring my wife the most joy?" or "God, please bring to mind a fun activity that the kids would really enjoy."

If you are not already regularly inquiring of the Lord, consider starting now. He wants this type of relationship with you. I encourage you to ask Him questions throughout your day and make space to listen to what He is saying. Inquiring of God becomes the platform to deepen our friendship with Him because it is not primarily about wanting information but seeking to be one that truly knows Him, understands His ways, and walks in a relationship with Him.

REVIEW

The first component of your spirit tank is prayer. In this chapter I introduced and busted the three prayer myths: that prayer is boring, that prayer is only for emergencies, and that prayer is ineffective. Make sure to prioritize prayer during a time you are mentally alert and physically rested, in a place where you can comfortably focus on Him.

To give you a simple plan on how to pray, I introduced the acronym ACTS. This type of prayer has you start with *adoration* and worship of the Lord, *confession* of any sin, giving *thanks* to God for all he has done, and ends with *supplication*—humbly laying your requests before God.

I ended the chapter introducing additional methods of prayer: intercession (or praying for others), prophetic prayer (praying for someone and sharing what God says with them), fasting (forgoing food or media for a period of time so you can focus on God), and inquiring of God (or asking God for guidance).

WHOLE LIFE CHALLENGE

As we bring prayer into the daily rhythms of our lives, I encourage you, for this chapter's Whole Life challenge, to make a commitment to spend fifteen minutes a day in conversation with God. Begin by finding your time and place to meet with God. Find a way to focus in on His presence. If you don't know where to start, focus on the acronym ACTS. Spend time in adoration, confess any sin, and then thank God for all He has done for you. Finally, pick one to three specific needs that you have, asking God to help meet the needs. Your needs could be anything: a desire for physical healing, the restoration of a broken relationship, or the ability to find a new job. Simply lift up what's been weighing on your heart. Be specific, and write your requests down in a prominent place—for example, a sticky note in the back of your Bible, or an index card taped to your bathroom mirror, or even a daily journal. This will remind you to bring your requests before God in prayer each day until you begin to see Him work in the situations you've written down or give you the direction you need.

Bible

three

Bible—A Gift from Above

*It ain't those parts of the Bible that I can't understand
that bother me, it's the parts that I do understand.*
—Mark Twain

*All Scripture is God-breathed and is useful for teaching, rebuking,
correcting and training in righteousness, so that the servant
of God may be thoroughly equipped for every good work.*
—The Apostle Paul, 2 Timothy 3:16–17

My grandmother died unexpectedly of an aneurism during the Thanksgiving break of my eighth-grade year. We were all devastated; she was a woman who poured her whole life into loving our family well. Her absence left a great hole in our lives. My grandmother's eyes lit up every year with the mention of Christmas. She loved when the family was together and able to take the time to simply enjoy each other, but she also loved celebrating Jesus' birth in a big way. She started planning months in advance, picking out presents for me and my younger sister and brother. She even had one of those old fake snow-covered trees that she put in her living room. That year was no exception. In fact, by the time of her passing, she had already wrapped two of my presents, but I, unfortunately, received only one of them.

The present I opened from her was a video game that I couldn't bring myself to play. To me, it represented the pain of losing her. For years I thought that video game was all I had left to remember her by.

During my sophomore year of college, my mom decided to clean out our attic. She came across the other gift, a huge plastic tote box my grandmother had assembled. While heading out the door for six months of studies in Utah, my mom packed the plastic tote from my grandmother in my truck.

I opened the tote when I arrived in Utah. Inside were over fifty of my grandmother's favorite Christian books. I was overcome with a bittersweet nostalgia for the visits to her house, seeing her read those very books, and listening to her stories about what God had done in her life.

I wasn't sure what to do with the books. They had a sentimental value to me, but I wasn't interested in Christianity or the Bible at the time. Nonetheless, I felt a connection to her through her notes in the books' margins. That tote full of books became a belated Christmas gift from a woman I loved dearly. It was a special gift that led me to one of the greatest gifts of all time: the Bible.

Up until that point, I had basically rejected my Christian roots, dismissed the Bible as irrelevant to my life, and begun to explore other religions. It was in that tote that I found Norman Vincent Peale's book *The Power of Positive Thinking*, which became the bridge for me to understand how practical and applicable the Bible could be.

Shortly after reading that book, I started paging through the book of Proverbs in the orange Gideon Bible I mentioned earlier. I found myself excited to continue reading the book that I had previously written off as old-fashioned and obsolete. Looking back, I realize that reading the scriptures in *The Power of Positive Thinking* is what allowed me to open my heart to the Bible.

I am always amazed at God's timing. If I had opened the box of books on the Christmas of my eighth-grade year, I am confident I wouldn't have been interested in reading them. Out of respect for my grandmother, they probably would have ended up on a bookshelf at my parents' house, where they'd be gathering dust to this day. However, my mother found them and passed them to me at a time in my life when I was feeling more lost than I had ever been. After reading through numerous New Age philosophical works, self-help books, and religious texts, I was receptive to *anything* that I thought could help me escape the uncertainty and confusion that had become my reality. Only the Bible was able to shine a light bright enough to dispel that darkness from my life.

My journey through God's Word began that afternoon in Utah, and it became the catalyst in developing a personal relationship with God. After I returned home from Utah for my junior year at Louisiana State University, I worked as a courier for a law firm in Baton Rouge. I read my orange Gideon Bible on my lunch break every day. One of the secretaries there saw me carrying my Bible (it fit in my back pocket). At first, she assumed I was a Christian, but after a few conversations she realized I was a seeker who had not yet accepted Christ as my personal savior. Picking up on my interest in the Bible, she told me about a ministry at LSU where there were other college students who read their Bibles. *Young people read the Bible?* I thought only older people like my grandparents read the Bible. She had piqued my interest, and I had to check it out.

The college ministry was called Living Waters, a group of roughly fifty born-again believers led by a young pastor named Stovall Weems. I surrendered my life to Jesus shortly after becoming involved with the group, and was soon baptized. Reading the Bible not only led to the greatest decision I have ever made—accepting Christ into my life— but also it has become the single most valuable book in my life.

THE ALL-TIME BESTSELLER

The Bible has been a perennial bestseller year after year, a unique phenomenon not applicable to any other book in history. A conservative estimate from 2005 showed that Americans purchased approximately 25 million Bibles. That's more than *half a billion dollars' worth of Bibles*! According to the Barna Group, 47 percent of Americans read the Bible every week. Other research has found that 91 percent of American households own at least one Bible—and the average household owns four—which means that Bible publishers manage to sell 25 million copies a year of a book that almost everybody already has.[1]

Why do Americans continue to buy copies of the Bible, even when they already own several? Doug Birdsall, president of American Bible Society, sees it as a problem similar to obesity in America: "We have an awful lot of people who realize they're overweight, but they don't follow a diet." He compared buying a new Bible with a different type of cover or different type of commentary to provide fresh motivation, similar to what most people feel when they start a new diet plan. People believe the Bible has value but they don't read it. If they do read it, the majority (57 percent) read their Bibles four times a year or less. Only 26 percent of Americans said they read their Bible on a regular basis.[2]

There is a big disconnect between owning Bibles and actually reading God's Word for the purpose of personal application and spiritual formation. Most people have a high respect or reverence for the Bible, but if they are honest, they will admit they have no intention of regularly reading it. Others who own Bibles have the desire to read and study the Bible, but they feel insecure about their lack of knowledge of the Bible and often don't know where to start.

I can relate to feeling intimidated about reading the Bible. I have been to seminary, and there are still many parts of it I am trying to wrap my mind around, but that doesn't keep me from working at it every day. I have learned to approach God's Word with the confident expectation that He will speak to me in the way I most need in that moment, and it's a promise you can apply to your life, too.

There are three main ways in which a person benefits from reading the Bible on a daily basis:

SPIRITUAL FOOD

The Bible is meant to be food for our spirits. In Deuteronomy 8:1–3 God reminded the people of Israel of His faithfulness to them during their forty years in the wilderness by feeding them manna *every day*. The purpose was to humble them and teach them that "man does not live on bread alone but on every word that comes from the mouth of the Lord" (verse 3).

In this story, the dry, lifeless wilderness was the place where the tribe of Israel was tested to see how much they trusted God to provide nourishment and direction in their daily lives: "God led you all the way in the wilderness these forty years, to humble and test you in order to know what was in your heart, whether or not you would keep his commands" (verse 2).

Unfortunately, the Israelites did not follow His instructions or seek the spiritual sustenance He wanted to give them. A whole generation of Israelites died in the wilderness instead of entering into the Promised Land because they failed to allow God's Word to sustain them. Their focus on achieving their shallow physical desires distracted them from the fact that God was trying to meet their deepest spiritual needs.

In Matthew 4:1–4, Jesus was tested in a similar way: He was led by the Spirit into the desert to be tempted, where He discovered that God's Word fed him and provided strength in a way that food could not. After fasting for forty days and forty nights, Jesus was *hungry*. At that point, Satan challenged Jesus by tempting Him to turn stones into bread. Jesus answered Satan, "It is written: 'Man shall not live on bread alone, but on every word that comes from the mouth of God'" (verse 4).

Where the Israelites failed in the wilderness, Jesus succeeded. I believe the words the Father spoke over Jesus right before He entered the wilderness were His source of strength: "This is my beloved Son, in whom I am well pleased" (Matthew 3:17). These words also revealed His true identity as God's Son. In a similar way, I believe God's Word is meant to play a similar role in our lives, to not only strengthen and sustain us, but to call us into our truest identity as loved sons and daughters of our Father God.

SPIRITUAL DIRECTION

The Bible is also meant to be a source of God's direction and guidance in our lives. When people tell me they aren't hearing from God about a question they've asked Him, I encourage them to spend some time in the Word. God loves to give direction through His Word as the Holy Spirit leads us to the very place where the answer lies.

God first spoke to me through a still, small voice in 1998 when He called me to plant a church in our nation's capital. In 2005 that same still, small voice told me that this church would one day have seventeen campuses in the D.C. Metro area and three in New York. With a business background and a decade of ministry experience, I knew the importance of having a vision for both the direction and mission of the church. I wanted God to tell me how to develop these campuses rather than craft them from my own ideas. And He did, through the book of Nehemiah.

As I read Nehemiah, I began to see the parallels between Jerusalem and the Washington D.C. area. The book of Nehemiah was written during a time when the Israelites were captives in Babylon. Nehemiah's heart was stirred for his capital, Jerusalem, a once thriving spiritual city where people came to worship God in the temple. When the Israelites were taken into captivity, Jerusalem was burned and became desolate. Nehemiah felt called not only to rebuild the physical walls around the city but to be a catalyst to help reestablish temple worship in the city.

Reading Nehemiah, I heard God say that, just as He called Nehemiah to rebuild the physical walls around the city, He was calling

Metro Church to partner with other churches in the area to rebuild the spiritual walls around the city of Washington, D.C. Our original vision "to build a God-first culture throughout the D.C. Metro area" and our mission "to build a God-first, multicultural church, meeting in multiple locations, that influences the culture one person at a time" both came from studying the book of Nehemiah and our desire to partner with God to rebuild a culture where He is loved, honored, and placed first. His message through His Word was clear to me, and Metro Church is now part of a circle of churches around our nation's capital that are helping to establish a God-first culture throughout the D.C. area.

God wants to speak to you through His Word. Whether to reveal your next steps in life or to give encouragement in an area where He wants you to grow, He's ready to speak to you and provide the help you need.

SPIRITUAL POWER

The Bible is an undeniable source of power in our lives. Hebrews 4:12 says, "For the word of God is alive and active. Sharper than any double-edged sword, it penetrates even to dividing soul and spirit, joints and marrow; it judges the thoughts and attitudes of the heart."

One night during my senior year of college, I heard a loud banging on my apartment door. I opened the door to find Andee, my first cousin, with a panicked look on her face. She was frantically motioning at a guy standing next to her who appeared to be drunk. She whispered to me, "I have been praying for him for hours, and I think I got six of the demons out, but there is one left, so I brought him here so you can help me."

My first thought was that I had misheard her. It's not every day that someone shows up at your doorstep saying they need your help getting a demon out of someone. And then the terrifying thought followed: *Why did you bring him to me?* The next thing I knew, we had led the guy to my futon and prayed for him to be free of any demonic influence in the name of Jesus. I definitely did not know what I was doing. In fact, I reverted back to what I remember the priest doing in the movie *The Exorcist.*

I am still not sure how it happened, but after Andee and I quoted Scripture over the man (at her direction) and prayed for him, he seemed suddenly and noticeably better. His eyes, which had rolled to the back of his head only minutes before, became normal; his thoughts, which had been nonsensical, suddenly became lucid. When combined with faith, God's Word becomes a vibrant and powerful force in our lives.

About three years later I spoke at a youth conference in my hometown of Lake Charles, Louisiana, and told the story of my participation in this living room exorcism. I was encouraging the youth leaders, letting them know that they have power, in Jesus' name, to overcome the enemy. Mid-message, I looked up to see a man approaching the stage. He boldly walked onto the stage and asked me for the microphone. I was so stunned I gave him the microphone. He said, "David doesn't know I'm here, but I am actually the guy he is talking about."

He explained that he had been experiencing a heaviness and confusion that he didn't know how to get free from, but after that visit to my apartment, he was set free of all demonic oppression and was now living a successful Christian life. The whole place was aghast and you could feel the faith level rising in the room. How could this have happened, the exact night that I'm delivering a message with this story in it? How could the main character of the story be in attendance? It quickly became clear to all of us it was not a coincidence. God was making himself known.

I believe we experienced the power of God's Word and prayer at work in this young man. As we quoted Scripture and prayed over him, something took place in the spiritual realm that caused the demonic influence oppressing him to flee.

While I don't deliver someone from demon possession every day, it is evident that there is real spiritual power in the Word. Second Corinthians 10:3–5 tells us that the weapons we fight with are not of the world, but they have divine power to demolish spiritual strongholds. I encourage you to ask God how He wants you to use His Word in your life as a source of His power.

WHERE TO START?

If you don't already own a Bible, find a version that you are comfortable reading. There are multiple versions of the Bible available, from the King James with its formal usage of the English language to modern versions with updated language. I use different versions when I prepare a sermon, but I favor the New International Version (NIV) for my daily reading.

If you want to read the Bible daily, develop a plan. Some people use an online plan to read through the Old or New Testament in a year, where there are assigned passages to read each day. If you want a more focused study, choose a book of the Bible to read, do a character study about one of the great men or women in the Bible, or do a study on a topic that interests you.

For a character study, look up the name of the person you choose to study in a concordance. A concordance is a book that helps you locate topics, words, or people throughout the Bible. Some stories of Bible characters are spread out over many chapters, and some Old Testament characters are even referenced in the New Testament. For example, if you want to research Abraham, a concordance will show you that the stories of Abraham are in Genesis chapters 12–25. He also is referenced in the New Testament twenty-two times. For example, in John 8:56–58 Jesus references Abraham when He says, "'Your father Abraham rejoiced at the thought of seeing my day; he saw it and was glad.' 'You are not yet fifty years old,' they said to him, 'and you have seen Abraham!' 'Very truly I tell you,' Jesus answered, 'before Abraham was born, I am!' "(NASB).

For a topical study, go to a concordance and search for the passages about that topic (marriage, family, money, relationships, heaven, purpose, etc.). If you are researching the topic of money, you might be surprised to find that money is mentioned about eight hundred times in the Bible or that Jesus taught that we are to pay our taxes and that we should exercise careful money management. Many study Bibles have concordances in the back, you can purchase a bound concordance at a bookstore, or you can find a few incredible concordances online. (I've listed a couple in the appendix.)

Sometimes the simplest way to start enjoying your Bible time is to cherry-pick a good story that looks interesting and dive in over the course of several days. I like to read some of the same old stories over and over—the ones that you saw up on the felt board in Sunday school. God can always bring out new insights and interpretations in something that seems familiar or old to us.

Some of my favorite stories in the Old Testament are that of David in First and Second Samuel, or the book of Joshua, in which the children of Israel finally come out of the desert and cross the Jordan River during its flood stage! In the New Testament, I love to revisit the book of Acts, which takes you through the birth of the Christian church, and the book of Mark, which talks about more demon possessions than any other book in the Bible. Talk about exciting!

As you read the section, topic, or story in the Bible you have chosen to study, ask questions about what you are reading. Ask about the historical context, when and to whom the passage(s) were written, and why it was written. Try to understand the context for the passage(s): Was there a specific need or issue that was being addressed? What type of literature is it: historical narrative, poetry, prophecy, or letters? First, read the whole book or the context surrounding the passage. If your questions are not answered, do an online search on the topic, passage, or setting of the book. For example, *Who were the*

Thessalonians at the time Paul wrote his letters to them? I also recommend Biblestudytools.com as an additional resource, which has theologians' comments on different passages and individual scriptures in the Bible.

Keep track of repeated terms or phrases as you read, and ask why they might be significant. When you come across theological terms that you are not familiar with, look them up to find out what they mean. Inquire about the overall theme of each passage. Keep searching for deeper meanings in each passage, and God will continue to reveal new insights to you every time you study the Bible.

To keep track of all your questions, record them in a notebook, on your phone, or on another device. As you find answers to your questions, write them next to the original question for future reference. As you gain a greater understanding about the book of the Bible, person, or topic you chose to study, ask what timeless principles you've learned that you can apply to your personal life. Applying what you study to your current situation is where the Word of God becomes spiritual food, direction, and a source of spiritual power in your life!

Remember, the key to the Whole Life plan is to find your own personal rhythm during each step, so find a way to study the Word of God that's enjoyable for you!

REVIEW

The Bible is the second main component in your spiritual formation as you seek to live in rhythm with God's plan. The Bible, when read and applied to daily living, brings about personal transformation. I shared how I found my own rhythm in Bible reading and how to sustain yours at a healthy level in your own Whole Life plan.

In this chapter, I also talked about how the Bible is the primary source of spiritual food, spiritual direction, and spiritual power in the life of a Christian. By reading it as a part of your daily spiritual formation regimen, you, too, can find consistent victory for living within its pages.

WHOLE LIFE CHALLENGE

If you are new to Bible reading, I encourage you to add it to your daily time with God. Find a version of the Bible that you are comfortable reading and decide your focus. Do you crave to know God's thoughts on a certain topic, or does a character study sound more appealing to you?

If you've already established daily time with God, challenge yourself to read through the Old or New Testament in a year. Get a notebook or utilize one of your electronic devices to record your questions and research about what you are reading.

In the chapter on prayer I encouraged you to start with fifteen minutes of time with God each day. Adding Bible study to that time will naturally increase your daily devotional time with God to twenty or twenty-five minutes. As you begin to discover the benefits of the Word of God and its application to your life, I can assure you the extra time will fly by.

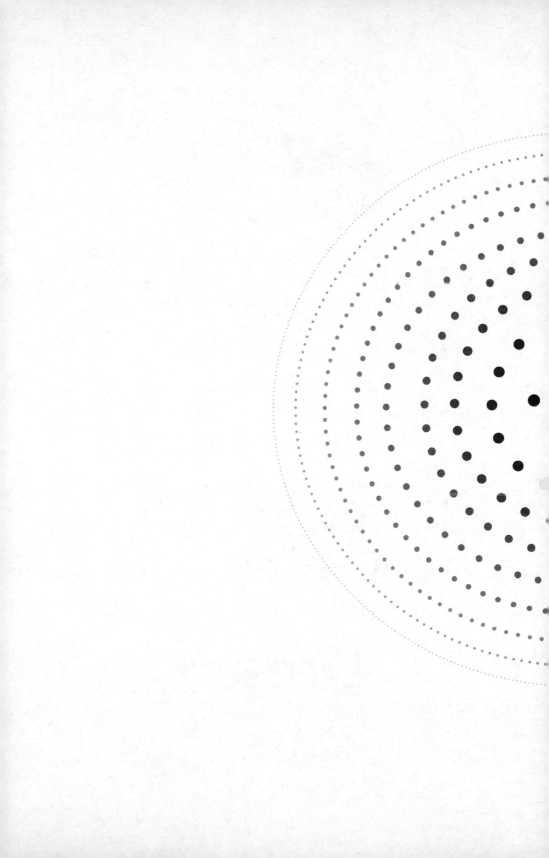

Dream

four

Dream—Discovering Your Purpose

I have a dream...
—Dr. Martin Luther King Jr.

*During the night the mystery was revealed to Daniel
in a vision. Then Daniel praised the God of heaven.*
—Daniel 2:19

The words "I have a dream" echoed across the Washington Mall on August 28, 1963: "I have a dream that my four little children will one day live in a nation where they will not be judged by the color of their skin but by the content of their character ... I have a dream today...." I believe the dream Dr. King articulated that day came from God's heart—and that Dr. King was placed on this earth to help bring it to pass. It was his purpose.

I also believe there are big dreams in God's heart that each of us have been placed on earth to help bring to pass—our purpose in life. To round out the spiritual formation section, we are going to focus on what it means to seek God's purpose for us in this season of your life. We will also discuss how to remain loyal to His purpose for you even when the circumstances are challenging. As we dream with God and walk toward the unfolding purpose He has for us, we deepen our relationship with Him and fill up our spirit tanks.

When you are on the path toward discovering God's purpose for this season of your life, you embark on an adventure with God. He doesn't always send a bolt of lightning and show us what the purpose is. More often than not, it's a scavenger hunt; we end up with clues in life that lead us to each piece of the puzzle. As each piece is added, the picture or dream becomes clearer and clearer. As Martin Luther King Jr. aptly observed, "Take the first step in faith. You don't have to see the whole staircase, just take the first step."[1]

Drawing from this advice, don't worry about stepping into the unknown. Take what you do know and make that the first step. And don't worry if you don't have a clear dream of the same magnitude as Martin Luther King Jr.'s. I doubt he knew the enormity of his dream when he first received it or understood how his words would be used to shape the course of history. You're only responsible for seeking God's direction and taking the next step He shows you. Psalm 32:8 tells us that He will guide us and direct us in the way we should go. As we follow Him, our dream, once clarified, becomes His invitation to play our unique part in His larger story.

My hope for you is that you discover and walk in God's purpose for you as a result of finding your Whole Life rhythm.

HOW TO DISCOVER YOUR DREAM

Clearly Dr. King had an overarching dream for his life. Even his name, Martin Luther—the reformer of the Protestant Reformation—spoke to his dream and purpose. But within his overarching dream there were different seasonal expressions that he lived out. Early on in his life he was bringing individual reformation to people as a pastor by helping them to reform the way they understood God. He also had seasons in his dream as a parent and spouse.

Just like Dr. King, you and I will have an overarching dream, but also different expressions of that dream depending on the season of life we are in. You may already have a promise or clear dream from God in your life. You know you want to start a business, develop your employees as leaders, provide a valuable product, or have abundant financial resources to sow back into God's Kingdom.

You may have a vision for raising a family where all your children walk closely with the Lord and impact His Kingdom in whatever sphere they are called to serve. Perhaps you have a dream to impact a part of society through your service as a doctor, judge, teacher, missionary, writer, police officer, artist, senator, or nonprofit director. Or potentially you are in between seasons or you are moving into a new season, and you need to clarify exactly where you are in God's plan to better partner with Him in the unfolding components of your dream. If your dream and purpose is clear, great! If not, I want to help you identify your dream, recognize where you are in the process, and navigate each step well.

PRAY FOR A PICTURE OF YOUR DREAM

If you don't know what your dream is, I encourage you to pray for a picture. Close your eyes and ask God to give you a mental image of where He is leading you. Joseph, the one with the multicolored coat, received a picture in the form of a dream. I believe this picture acted as a great source of encouragement in his life when he went through trying seasons and reminded him that his story was not over.

Sometimes we receive a picture immediately. Other times it takes a while to receive a dream that resonates with us. Either way, when we receive a picture, we should begin to pray about it and ask God who we should share it with and how we can position ourselves for the dream's unfolding. A few years ago I saw a very vivid picture of me and my wife, Taryn, in our front yard on a swing. As I prayed over her and our marriage, I saw what looked like a Google Earth aerial view from heaven and then gradually began to zoom in on our front yard. In the picture, I had my arm around Taryn and we were filled with joy over all that God had brought to pass in our lives. (I could tell it was many years in the future, because my hair was much longer and grayer than it actually was at the time.) The thing that stood out to me most in this picture was how happy we were.

I am not sure of the full meaning of what I saw, but I believe it is a picture of the incredible marriage that God has for Taryn and me and a reminder that He has significant things He wants to do through us as a couple. After I received this picture, I became even more intentional in my relationship with Taryn and renewed my focus to significantly invest in our marriage. I shared it with Taryn, and we both committed to pray over the picture and ask God for any other proactive steps we needed to take so that the vision would come to pass. I shared this picture in a message at church, and a young man who served as an usher at church offered to build a swing for us in our front yard. We accepted his generous offer, and he built us a swing identical to the one I saw in my picture. That picture continues to infuse us with hope in the more trying seasons of our marriage and reminds us to not settle until we fully experience all the good things that God has for us together. We are intentionally positioning ourselves to walk toward the picture. We have since moved from the house where the swing was built, but we have a new image of our future together through that swing, and we often recall it to each other as part of God's promise for us during our nightly prayer walk we take together.

If you don't receive a picture in your mind right away, I encourage you to keep asking and not give up. Sometimes it comes after a few days or even weeks. If you receive a picture and you are not sure if it is from God or your own imagination, share it with a close Christian friend who can help you discern the potential meaning and pray with you for God's clarity and confirmation. I always encourage those coming to me for counsel to make sure the picture agrees with Scripture. God is not going to ask us to do something that contradicts what He has already instructed us in His Word. Colossians 3:15 says, "Let the peace of Christ rule in your hearts . . ." so I also examine whether I sense the peace and presence of God over the picture that I received.

We don't always understand the full meaning of our dream when we receive it, so I recommend asking God to continue to lead you each step of the way and ask Him if there is anything that you should do to partner with Him. For example, I don't think that Joseph understood the full significance of his picture until over a decade later, when his brothers came to him in their time of need. By that time he had become second to Pharaoh, and Joseph's sphere of leadership was probably larger than he ever imagined back when he received the dream.

Because of our innate desire to be in control, I am confident that God wants to lead us more than we want to be led. So, as He makes your path clear, resist the temptation to get ahead of Him. If your heart is to follow Him, He will bring understanding about what you need to know or do at exactly the right time.

DISCOVER YOUR DREAM WHILE SERVING

If you don't receive a picture like Joseph did, don't be concerned. There are multiple ways God shows us our purpose. The most important thing to remember is to have a willing heart with no conditions. Fully surrendering to His will creates the environment needed for us to clearly see what He wants us to do and when He wants us to act. Praying for God to do something great with our lives is a prayer He always answers. But prayer alone isn't always enough: our overall spiritual condition needs to be active and strong. A recommendation I often make is to serve someone else's God-first dream while they are waiting for clarity on their own dream. Your church is a great place to start. Discover the vision of the lead pastor and brainstorm how you can further that vision. Find a ministry or outreach that stirs your heart and use the gifts God has given you to help steward their mission.

By serving another's purpose and dream, you will better understand yours. As you serve, God will use other people to confirm or affirm who you are and who He created you to be. He will often use this time to reveal areas in your life that need more development or show the way in which your spirit, soul, or body is out of alignment.

There are three primary areas of influence that affect how you serve and give clarity about your calling: your gifts, your burden, and your experience. When you find an area of service where those gifts, burden, and experience overlap, that is a good sign it is an area where God is calling you.

1. Gifts

First Corinthians 12:7 communicates that all believers have been given gifts "given for the common good." If you don't know what your gifts are, it's very likely your church has a test you can take. There are also free tests and excellent books on the subject available. (See the appendix for a couple suggestions.) But a good place to start is to simply think about what you're naturally good at and what you do that receives praise from others. These are clues that show where God can and wants to use you.

If you take one of the gift tests, you'll probably discover that you have more than one gift, and you will find you score stronger on some gifts than others. There are gifts ranging from leadership, compassion, and exhortation (motivational speaking) to carpentry, teaching, and being a good listener. After you identify your gifts, write down your top five and focus on developing these. I personally like the book *StrengthsFinder 2.0*[2] by Tom Rath because it identifies your top five gifts, referred to as strengths, as they relate to each other.

Another thing I like about *StrengthsFinder 2.0* is that each copy has a unique password in the back that allows you to take their version of the test online. It identifies thirty-four different strengths in four general categories. When you take the test online, it gives you your top five strengths. I have used it extensively when coaching leadership teams, consulting with businesses, even training my own staff. The main premise is that by focusing on your strengths as opposed to your weaknesses, you can improve by leaps and bounds in the area that you are naturally strong.

2. Burden

A burden is like a call of duty and can be defined as something that moves you to action. What issue or group of people burdens your heart? Maybe it is a cause like wanting to stop human trafficking. Maybe it is a particular demographic that you feel called to minister to, like high school students, children, or the elderly. Issues that stir your spirit, cause your adrenaline to race, or make your blood boil can be clues to discovering where God is calling you to be a part of the solution. Maybe you get upset whenever you hear about adult illiteracy because God is calling you to help educate those who somehow slipped through the cracks of our education system. Maybe you get angry whenever you hear about the rising state of homelessness in your town because God is calling you to help those marginalized in society to have a roof over their head and to feel valued.

In the process of discovering your dream, it is important to take inventory of the things in your life that move you to take action. For me, I knew I wanted to plant a church, and when it came to finding the right city for planting, my heart consistently defaulted to our nation's capital. I felt a church in the D.C. area could truly benefit the entire country and wanted to serve and pastor to those who shape our nation. It was a true call of duty.

3. Experience

What experience do you have? In *The Hiding Place*, Corrie ten Boom wisely observed, "Every experience God gives us, every person He puts in our lives is the perfect preparation for the future that only He can see."[3] Your experience could be a job skill you have, like fixing cars or cooking gourmet meals, but it could also be something harder you walked through, like a divorce or an illness. God will use both our skills and our circumstances as preparation for where He is calling us, so it is helpful to reflect on these and ask Him how He wants to use them for His bigger purpose. His purpose for you is often revealed through a compilation of your past and current experiences. For me, I had experienced many different ministry expressions and had a business degree in entrepreneurship, so it seemed fitting to marry the two experiences together by starting a ministry.

The Venn diagram is an excellent tool to see where your gifts, burdens, and experiences meet to form your unique dream and purpose. On the Venn diagram below, fill in each section and see which gifts, burdens, and experiences overlap. For example, if you have a gift of teaching, a call of duty to help rear young children, and you've taught Sunday school the past year, they intersect around the area of teaching children.

Perhaps you have a burden for the homeless in your city, a gift of administration, and experience organizing large activities at work. Perhaps part of your dream is organizing outreach activities—meals, clothing distribution, or health services—to the homeless community.

Not everything you fill in each of the three areas of gift, burden, and experience will intersect—so don't force them together. But where there is a natural intersect, take notice: It may be a confirmation of part of God's purpose for you.

BURDEN

EXPERIENCE   GIFT

PROMISE, PROBLEM, AND PROVISION CYCLE

When I examined the lives of men and women in Scripture who lived out their dream, I noticed a clear pattern. First, they received a prophetic promise from God or a foreshadowing of what was to come. Next, there was either a problem or a series of challenges they had to overcome. Finally, after years of waiting and growing, provision came. Once I identified this pattern, I observed how these men and women held on to their promise and remained faithful in spite of long seasons of problems. I believe this biblical pattern will prove helpful to you as you seek to pursue your dream and remain unshaken in the midst of apparent delays and detours.

Genesis 37:5–8 explains that Joseph had a dream about his purpose. In his dream, Joseph and his brothers were binding sheaves of grain in the field, when Joseph's sheaf rose and stood upright and his brothers' sheaves gathered around his and bowed down. Understandably, when Joseph shared this dream with his brothers, they hated him more than ever. They all understood that Joseph's dream was about him ruling over them, and his brothers had no desire or intention of bowing down to him! While Joseph understood the meaning of the dream, I'm sure he had no idea how significant it would be. He didn't realize the dream was about a call to government leadership that God had placed on his life, and he didn't know how God would bring this dream to pass.

After he received his dream, Joseph encountered a plethora of problems, which can be read about in Genesis chapters 37–50. His brothers threw him into a pit; sold him as a slave to Midianite merchants, who ultimately sold him to a wealthy, powerful man named Potiphar; and then went home and told their parents that Joseph had been murdered. Joseph, who remained very devoted to God through it all, was wrongly accused of making a pass at Potiphar's wife and thrown into prison. In prison, the warden put Joseph in charge of the other prisoners, which was the first fulfillment of Joseph's call to leadership—but he was still in prison. He had a friend who was released from prison and was supposed to put in a good word about Joseph to Potiphar, but the friend forgot, so Joseph remained there for another two years. I imagine Joseph was filled with doubt and wondered if his dream would ever come to pass.

In the meantime, God's providential hand brought the next big step: Pharaoh wanted an interpreter for a dream he had had, and Joseph was the only person who could do it. Pharaoh was so impressed and grateful that he put Joseph as second in charge of all of Egypt—a significant promotion! Things came full circle when Joseph's brothers came to buy grain from Egypt because of the famine. It had been over a decade since they had seen Joseph, so while Joseph recognized them, they did not recognize him. When they approached Joseph, they bowed down to honor him because of his place of leadership, and thus the prophetic dream became a reality.

The revelation of a dream and the fulfillment of that purpose can be separated by a length of time as well as several unpredictable events, as we see in Joseph's story. Nonetheless, hold on to the dream about the purpose that God has given you. I often tell people that when God gives you a dream, hold on tight to it, because He knew you would need it for the road ahead. The cycle, as described below, is the practical application of God fulfilling the dream.

Promise

Your promise could be a picture given to you, or it could be the clarified dream you are feeling led to invest in after examining your gifts, burdens, and experiences. It is essentially where you think you are headed in the vision God has given you in this season of your life.

In Genesis 12:1–3, God clearly gives Abraham a promise when He tells him to leave his country, people, and family for a new land—where Abraham's descendants, God's chosen people, would become a great nation. The absurdity was that Abraham was around seventy-five and his wife Sarah was sixty-five years old and barren. Can you imagine receiving this promise when you have gray hair and dentures? They were already well past the typical child-bearing age, so the promise seemed impossible. Sarah laughed when she first heard it, and they both struggled to believe how it would become a reality.

Problem

After you receive your promise or after you pinpoint your purpose, you can be sure to expect some problems. These problems can last a few months or they can last many years, as we saw with Joseph. This part of the cycle is often made up of delays, detours, and difficulties before deliverance comes. The important thing to remember during these times is to keep your eyes on the dream and the One who gave it to you. "Being confident of this, that he who began a good work in you will carry it on to completion until the day of Christ Jesus" (Philippians 1:6).

Here are three common types of problems we experience when we pursue our purpose.

✦ Delay

Sarah was barren when she received the promise. Several years later, in Genesis 16:1, she was still without children. We have all experienced delays in life—delays in traffic, delays at the doctor's office, delays at work. Delays are unfortunately a part of life. When there is a delay, the temptation to start questioning or wondering if you misheard God will arise. This is where you need to draw close to God, remember the dream He gave you, and move forward in faith with Him.

✦ Detour

When there is a delay in fulfilling our dream, it becomes tempting to take matters into our own hands. When we do that, we take a detour from God's plan. This is exactly what happened with Abraham and Sarah.

Sarah got tired of waiting, so she had an Egyptian slave named Hagar lay with Abraham to conceive a child. That was obviously not God's idea, and there were consequences for their son, Ishmael: "He will be a wild donkey of a man; his hand will be against everyone and everyone's hand against him, and he will live in hostility toward all his brothers" (Genesis 16:12).

✦ Difficulty

Twenty-five years after Abraham and Sarah received the promise that they'd have a child, there was still no child of their own and no sign of a child coming. Genesis 17:17 says, "Abraham fell facedown; he laughed and said to himself, 'Will a son be born to a man a hundred years old? Will Sarah bear a child at the age of ninety?'" He was having trouble believing that he could really trust God's promise.

After waiting twenty-five years, Sarah finally became pregnant and had a son named Isaac. He was the fruition of their long-awaited promise, so it seemed totally illogical and counterintuitive when in Genesis 22:2 God told Abraham to take his only son Isaac to the region of Moriah, and prepare to sacrifice him as a burnt offering on one of the mountains.

_____

During the problem stage, many of us have found ourselves in a season of waiting when there is a delay or difficulty, or a combination of the two. If you are in that situation now, I know it can be a really challenging season. It can seem as though things are never going to turn around. From someone who has sat in his fair share of waiting rooms, I want to encourage you that your breakthrough will come! Here are some things I suggest doing while you are in a season of waiting on the Lord:

1. Remember the Power of Faith

Romans 4:16 reminds us, "Therefore, the promise comes by faith . . ." We see from Abraham and Sarah's example that there is a process of faith involved in receiving a promise. God often gives us the promise or dream years before it will come to pass. And as we wait, and remain faithful to Him, He works in our lives to prepare us for our purpose. The hidden power to keep the faith, although intangible, can prove to be the ultimate game changer and give you hope while you are in the waiting room.

2. Recall What God Has Done for You

Romans 4:17 says that Abraham was "our father in the sight of God, in whom he believed—the God who gives life to the dead and calls into being things that were not." Remembering all that God has done is one of the best faith builders for truly believing that He is going to move again. Recalling just some of the things that God has done for you through the years can be a catalyst for gratitude and shifts your perspective toward what He is doing rather than focusing on what He is not doing.

3. Rely on God's Promises

Romans 4:18 reminds us, "Against all hope, Abraham in hope believed and so became the father of many nations, just as it had been said to him, 'So shall your offspring be.'" Abraham had many reasons to question the promise of God. He was about one hundred years old, had a body that was as good as dead, and a wife whose womb was dead. But, Romans 4:20 says, "he did not waver through unbelief regarding the promise of God, but was strengthened in his faith and gave glory to God . . ."

Like Abraham, you can be honest about your current circumstances but still stand upon God's promises and count on the fact that they will come to pass. The hard part is that you don't know when or how his promises will be fulfilled, but you can be sure of His faithfulness. Philippians 1:6 says, "[be] confident of this, that He who began a good work in you will carry it on to completion until the day of Christ Jesus."

4. Rejoice with Expectation

Romans 4:20–21 explains, "Yet [Abraham] did not waver through unbelief regarding the promise of God, but was strengthened in his faith and gave glory to God, being fully persuaded that God had power to do what he had promised." Abraham is a true hero of the faith. From his example, we learn that, in spite of all the obstacles, we can still stay in a place of joyful expectation. This can be difficult to do when we are at a low point, or not seeing God at work in our circumstances.

If you are finding the rejoicing with expectation difficult, think back over all that God has done in your past. Remember the times He provided or blessed or gave you the direction you needed at just the right time. What promises—more than six thousand in the Bible—has He fulfilled in your life? As you remember all that He has already done for you, begin to thank Him for past blessings, and then thank Him for what is to come. An attitude of rejoicing with expectation will help keep your focus on God, the One who can help you, instead of the difficult or impossible circumstances in front of you.

Provision

We all love happy endings! God gave Abraham and Sarah a son, and Abraham obeyed when God told him to sacrifice his son. As Abraham lifted the knife to kill Isaac, the Lord stopped him. Abraham then looked up and saw a ram caught by its horns in a thicket. So he took the ram and sacrificed it instead of his son. Abraham called that place "The Lord Will Provide." Because of Abraham's obedience, the Lord promised to bless Abraham, increase his descendants as much as the stars in the sky and the sand on the seashore, and bless all the nations of the earth through his offspring.

If you find it difficult to follow God, apply the two principles to your life that we see in Abraham's life: trust and obedience. When the promises of God don't make sense, trust the One who made the promises. God is a good Father, and you can trust Him even when you question His direction. And, like Abraham, obey God even in difficult times, knowing that your obedience will lead to provision in your life.

I am not sure where you are in your promise, problem, and provision cycle. If you are waiting for your provision, there are two primary types to watch for. The first is when a breakthrough happens. A breakthrough is when a positive change occurs in your negative circumstance. The second is when provision comes through a change in you. If you are not receiving a breakthrough, it could be either because the timing is not right or because God wants you to have a personal change before He delivers his promise to your circumstances.

As you position yourself to walk toward the clarified dream that is in your heart, stay faithful to pursue His purpose for you, because at the right time, and in the right way, He will bring a breakthrough. As Galatians 6:9 reminds us, "Let us not become weary in doing good, for at the proper time we will reap a harvest if we do not give up." Each time we walk through this cycle of promise, problem, and provision, our relationship with God deepens and He is glorified.

REVIEW

Each of us has a dream and purpose in this life. In this chapter I encouraged you with some of the ways we discover our dreams and the process we each go through to reach that dream. If you don't know your dream, you can pray that God will show you a picture of it, and also discover or better understand your dream through serving others. Your particular gifts, burdens for others, and experiences will likely converge as you serve and confirm your purpose.

I also introduced the promise, problem, and provision cycle, showing how a dream about purpose is usually met with problems—delays, detours, and difficulties—as we move toward the fulfillment of the dream. I also talked about how helpful it is to the process of faith when we know what stage we are at in this cycle. Knowing where we are will not only strengthen our faith but also help us to know how to better position ourselves before God in order to move on to a place of provision by Him.

As part of the problem stage, I talked about the waiting room, a season of delays where we need to remember the power of faith, recalculate what God has done for us, rely on God's promises, and rejoice with expectation. We all deal with problems as a part of the process of faith but there is something very powerful about understanding how to apply these practical applications to our waiting room experience.

WHOLE LIFE CHALLENGE

As our Whole Life challenge for this chapter, I encourage you to determine where you are on the promise, problem, and provision path. If you do not know your dream, what can you do to discover it? Perhaps you need to ask God for a picture of your dream, or maybe you need to find a place of service in your church or community where you can allow your gifts, burdens (personal calls of duty), and life experiences help define your purpose. Write down your top three dreams for this season of your life. Just like in the prior chapter, write them in a prominent place to see each day and make them a part of your daily devotional prayer time.

What are your gifts, burdens, and experiences? Take a minute to complete your own Venn diagram. Then determine what specific steps you can begin to take toward the intersection points on the diagram that reflect your dream and purpose.

If you are in the problem stage of the cycle, what are you experiencing: delays, detours, or difficulties? How does God want you to respond to the problems in your life so you will be fully prepared when He brings the provision for your dream? If you are in a season of waiting, how are you faithfully stewarding what God has given you? Are you helping others move forward in their dream while you patiently anticipate your own?

If you need some help with identifying your dream, or want some support during the problem stage, I encourage you to connect with your Whole Life partner or a close friend and share what is on your mind. Remember, our dream in this season of our lives is never just a one-person project.

part two

Soul Care

SOUL IS A POPULAR TERM in pop culture, especially in the South, where I grew up. There's soul food, which unfortunately doesn't make it on to the recommended food lists of most nutritionists. There are soul mates and even *Soul Train* (as in the infamous dance line or, better yet, the American music-dance TV show). If you enjoy a vacation to a scenic location, it is often described as "good for the soul." If you give all your effort to something, it is said that you "put your heart and soul into it."

Even though this term has become ubiquitous in our culture, many don't actually know what the soul is or how it is different from the spirit. I know *I* didn't have a clear understanding of the soul until I started to study Scripture. In this section, we will define the soul from a biblical perspective and learn how we can care for our souls so that we experience true and lasting transformation in our Whole Life journey.

Hebrews 4:12 talks about dividing the soul and the spirit, which implies that they are separate. While the human spirit gives us consciousness of God—our human spirits communing with His Spirit—our souls give us self-consciousness. With our souls we think and feel and make decisions. The two are very distinct and separate, although as I discussed in chapter one, both are critical to our overall health.

Our spirits and souls are the redeemed parts of our beings that will go to heaven one day. However, while our spirits are perfected at the point of our salvation, our souls definitely are not. Our minds, wills, and emotions are in the process of sanctification—a fancy theo-logical word meaning they are becoming whole and healed.

Experiencing transformation and ultimate wholeness in our souls is empowered by the Holy Spirit who lives in us when we accept Christ into our hearts—but we have a role to play and work to do on our part, too. This is where a lot of people—myself included—get stuck, because they don't know how to care for their souls. By the time of my burnout, the years of not paying attention to my negative emotions or thought patterns finally caught up with me, leaving me feeling unable to handle my responsibilities and relationships in a healthy way. In fact, 3 John 1:2 affirms this: "Beloved, I pray that in every way *you may prosper* and enjoy good health, *as your soul also prospers*" (emphasis mine, NASB). This is a strong statement that helps us to see God's desire for rhythm in our lives: *We prosper in life and experience health in our bodies when our soul prospers.* It's important to remember not only to look for the explicit meanings of a passage but to uncover the implicit wisdom Scripture also imparts. In this passage it clearly says we prosper and experience good health when our soul prospers, but it also implies the opposite: *When our souls are not cared for, we do not prosper in life, nor do our bodies remain healthy.* From this passage my eyes were opened to see that my soul was potentially in even more jeopardy than my body.

It is for this reason that the soul section of this book focuses on the three parts of the soul—mind, will, and emotions—and gives practical advice on how to care for these areas. The understanding of mind, will, and emotions was popularized by a twentieth-century Chinese believer Watchman Nee in *The Spiritual Man*. From Scrip-ture, Nee formulated the function of decision, thought, and feeling as the main functions of the human soul.

The mind is the source of all of our thoughts, good or bad, con-scious and subconscious. Our will is the source of our actions that execute our priorities. It influences the choices we make and what we do with our lives. Our emotions are our feelings, which can change countless times in the course of a single day. The soul is also where the personality resides. The soul is extremely interconnected in and of itself, and our thoughts (mind) have an enormous impact on what we do (will) and how we feel (emotions).

Over the past two years, I have heard more sermons about the importance of caring for your soul and the detriments of a neglected soul than in my previous twenty years of ministry combined. I think we are finally realizing that most crisis situations like burnout, affairs, or addiction occur because of fractures in the soul. I believe it is God's desire for each and every one of us to experience a soul that prospers.

In this section we will take an honest look at the current condition of our soul and learn how to implement exercises that will promote its health. The spiritual foundations we covered in the last section are not only ways to connect with God but also catalysts for greater health in the soul. We will build on these in the following chapters by first learning how to renew your mind through drawing from your true identity in Christ, and then exposing any ungodly beliefs you may have obtained up to this point in life. We'll learn to say yes to God-first priorities, and we'll learn to maintain healthy emotions while working through the less-than-ideal ones as we move to a place of wholeness in our souls.

the
whole
life

Mind

five

Mind—A Beautiful Mind

Change your thoughts and you change your life.
—Norman Vincent Peale

If my mind can conceive it, and my heart
can believe it—then I can achieve it.
—Muhammad Ali

Who has known the mind of the Lord so as
to instruct him? But we have the mind of Christ.
—The Apostle Paul, 1 Corinthians 2:16

One of my favorite Bible stories is the Parable of the Prodigal Son. It is a powerful story that symbolizes God's great love for us even when we rebel. In relation to our soul, the story also communicates the power of the mind and its influence on one man's life. The prodigal son made two decisions directly influenced by unhealthy thoughts. First, he decided he wanted to get out of his father's house and go experience what the Bible calls "wild living" in another country. Because he was unsatisfied with the life his father had provided for him and thought he could find fulfillment elsewhere, he requested his inheritance, and departed into his desired destiny.

After he spent all his money, the prodigal son was reduced to feeding pigs to make a living. A famine swept through the land at the same time, and the son became so hungry that he even considered eating the pigs' food himself. As soon as he recognized his miserable condition and remembered how good things had been back at his father's house, the Bible says "he came to his senses" (Luke 15:17) and decided to head home to see if he could perhaps work as a servant for his father.

This story illustrates that our thoughts influence our feelings and the decisions we make. When our minds think on what God desires, blessings follow. When our minds do not conform to God's will, unhealthy behaviors and bad decisions will manifest in our lives. If we try to change our behavior without careful examination of our thought life, we are setting ourselves up for an exercise in futility. Proverbs 23:7 says, "For as he has thought in his soul, so [is] he."[1] If we want to see any lasting change in our lives as we work toward a whole life, we have to first change the way we think and find ways to regain control over our thought patterns.

John Nash, an American mathematician whose life was depicted in *A Beautiful Mind*, was one such man who struggled to bring order to his thought life. Diagnosed with paranoid schizophrenia at age thirty-one, he began to confuse the fantasies of his own mind with reality. During the second half of his life, John learned how to master his erratic thoughts. Although some things remained unchanged in his life, he learned some simple techniques that helped him determine which thoughts were not based in fact. By the end of his life, he became so successful that he received a Nobel Prize in economics.

One of the things that helped John navigate the world effectively was learning to discern what was *real* from what was *false*. With his wife's help, he identified the imagined characters for what they were, "figments of his overactive imagination." He also identified the real characters who were present and held him accountable to truth. His wife, Alicia Nash, ended up becoming a real totem in his life that kept him grounded. Since our thoughts so easily affect our actions and determine if we reach our God-given dreams, it's incredibly important to learn to recognize whether the ideas that enter into our minds are true or false.

As believers, God has given us His Word as a litmus test to help us decipher the truth from the enemy's lies. Any thoughts that do not line up with God's Word have the potential to become *ungodly beliefs*—"all beliefs, decisions, attitudes, agreements, judgments, or expectations that do not agree with God (His Word, His nature, His character)."[2] As believers, we must learn to reject these ungodly thoughts because they do not align with God's truth about us, others, or Himself. We use the Word of God and the trusted advisors in our lives—spouses, close friends, pastors, or even your Whole Life partner—to expose ungodly beliefs. As we will learn in this chapter, ungodly beliefs need to be exposed, torn down, submitted to God, and replaced with godly beliefs.

First Corinthians 2:16 explains that we should have "the mind of Christ" reminding us of our call to focus on thoughts that line up with His truth. And Romans 8:29 tells us that, as believers, our goal is to be continually transformed into the image of Christ, which means we continue to become more and more like Him. The more we allow God to transform us, the more our minds become like His.

UNGODLY BELIEFS

To change how our minds think, we must first recognize any ungodly beliefs we are partnering with so we can proactively reject them. Years ago, after I had my epiphany on the importance of pursuing a whole life, I began to actively seek help for my weaker areas.

During one of my sabbaticals, a friend recommended a ministry called Restoring the Foundations to help address the depletion I was experiencing in my soul. This ministry provides an integrated biblical approach to healing, freedom from life's hurts, and renewed purpose for living, with the goal of enabling you to be all God created you to be.[3] That winter, Taryn and I drove to the mountains of Hendersonville, North Carolina, to take part in their program together. I had no idea what to expect.

What took place over the course of one week was quite incredible, as Taryn and I each heard from God in very specific ways on the topics of performing for affirmation, fear of man, and broken relationships. This was a profound process. I've found that when you hear God speak a truth into your life—even if you have known it cognitively for years—you receive a newfound empowerment to live that truth. Through the trust that was renewed in Him that fateful week, I have experienced His nearness and His love in deeper ways, even in the midst of very difficult circumstances.

Taryn and I both agreed that it was one of the best weeks for our relationship in the years we had been married. When our individual personal freedoms are strengthened, we know that it positively impacts our marriage, children, and church family. One of the most significant insights we had over this week was in the area of ungodly beliefs. Ungodly beliefs can be insidious and far-reaching, as they are usually buried deep within your soul. You can live what appears to be a happy, godly life, but when you get honest with yourself and allow God to reveal what you believe in certain areas, you discover there are lies that you have partnered with, often unknowingly, that don't align with God's Word.

Ungodly beliefs come in three major categories: a wrong belief about God, a wrong belief about self, and a wrong belief about others. Below are some of the many ungodly beliefs in each of the three categories, followed by three main ungodly beliefs that people deal with and how Taryn and I dealt with each one.

Common Ungodly Beliefs about God

+ God loves other people more than me.

+ God has forgotten me.

+ God can't be trusted. He has disappointed me in the past and He will do it again.

✦ God doesn't listen to my prayers.

✦ God values me for what I do. If I am not doing much, He is disappointed in me.

✦ God short-changed me in my looks, my intelligence (or whatever area you feel lacking). Therefore, I must not be as valuable as someone else who has what I don't.

Common Ungodly Beliefs about Self

✦ I'll never be able to fully give or receive love.

✦ If people really knew me, they wouldn't like me.

✦ My real value is in what I do, my successes, and what I can accomplish.

✦ I have messed up so much that I have missed God's plan for my life.

✦ I need to plan everything and be in control to avoid chaos or uncertainty.

✦ I will never meet anyone to marry. I am without hope and destined to be alone.

✦ I cannot change. I will always be . . .

Common Ungodly Beliefs about Others

✦ I need to be very guarded, because people aren't safe. The best way to avoid rejection is to isolate myself.

✦ Relationships are more trouble than they are worth. I don't really need to be in relationships with others.

✦ I need praise from others to feel good about myself.

+ Authority figures cannot be trusted.

+ We will always have a broken marriage.

+ If others accept or approve of me, I'll be okay.

UNGODLY BELIEF #1: The Performance Trap

Ungodly beliefs often enter through a hurt from our childhood or result from a tragic event. When we are wounded, we are susceptible to believing a lie that becomes rooted in our thought process and shapes our future behavior. The most damaging aspect of the painful events we experience in our lives is not the hurt we experience in the moment but rather the *wrong interpretations* we make about God, ourselves, or others as a result of the pain.

For example, the boy whose father never showed up for his sporting events not only is disappointed in the moment but forms ungodly beliefs that will negatively impact all his future relationships, such as *I'm not worth showing up for* and *People will always disappoint me*. Despite his early conditioning, he is not quite sure why he puts up walls to guard his heart from future rejection and never fully offers himself in his closest relationships. He will continue this pattern of fear of intimacy and low self-worth until he confronts these ungodly beliefs that unknowingly shape so much of his behaviors and relationships.

As another example, the little girl whose father did not give her attention or affirm her value can have lasting damage on her self-image and self-worth. Over time, that little girl can form ungodly beliefs that she is not worth spending time with. This obviously is not true from God's point of view, nor is it something that He would want any of His daughters to believe about themselves. To Him, every person, male or female, is cherished and adored.

My most ensnaring ungodly belief was in the area of performance, which entered my thought life when I was around eight years old and assigned to a remedial reading group. There were four different reading levels, and I was in the very lowest one. All my friends were in the top group or the second most advanced group. The other kids in the remedial group had very obvious learning challenges. I didn't have a learning disability, but reading was very hard for me. Because I stumbled and stuttered when my teacher called on me to read aloud, I avoided it like the plague. No one ever called me stupid, but I definitely don't remember being called smart like all my friends. I felt so ashamed of my struggles reading that I drew my own conclusions that something must be really wrong with me.

This ungodly belief followed me through middle school and high school. Consequently I became a master at trying to hide my insecurities and inadequacies from others in new settings. I studied for hours longer than my peers, believing that if I worked hard enough, then no one would find out I wasn't smart. I was also overzealous at becoming popular. I didn't realize it at the time, but I was expending an inordinate amount of effort to overcompensate for my supposed inadequacies and the feeling that I didn't have what it took to succeed in life. It was really quite exhausting.

In my sophomore year of high school, I reached my breaking point, deciding I couldn't keep up the façade to cover my insecurities anymore. However, I was still desperate for the approval of others, so I subconsciously came up with a new plan. I decided to become laser focused on the sport of tennis and channeled all my energy into trying to become a star athlete. It worked for a time, simply because of the accolades and sense of accomplishment I found in tennis. Soon my entire identity became wrapped up in my successes on the tennis court.

I was bound and determined to become a pro tennis player, so you can imagine my dismay when I tore my ACL in college, cutting my promising tennis career short. It felt like my world had come crashing in on me; everything I'd been living for was taken from me in a moment. At that point, not knowing what else to do, I joined a fraternity, diving head-first into a lifestyle of partying. My identity was destroyed, and the feelings of worthlessness immediately set in again.

When I encountered God's love and surrendered my life to Jesus during my junior year of college, I knew something had changed forever in my life. All my questioning had ceased in a moment and my heart had come alive. Overnight I made a decision to step fully away from my hard-partying lifestyle and resigned from the fraternity I had pledged.

In the coming weeks, all the old friends who crossed paths with me said the same thing: "You look different! What's going on? It seems like you are doing amazing." I had given up my partying lifestyle, and my friends could see the effects of the change in my life, but the same ungodly beliefs that had made me seek approval from others through the partying instead of God were still with me.

Whatever issues we come to Jesus with do not automatically disappear when we surrender our lives to Him. Even though I had completely ended my partying ways, my performance issue was still alive and well. After I came to Christ, it began to manifest in a different area of my life. My addiction to "being the best" took the form of attempting to be the best student in order to impress others. Underneath it all, I was still trying to hide the inadequacies I felt when I was all alone. This revelation was so shocking—yet it also made perfect sense.

SOLUTION #1: *Realizing Our Identity as a Loved Child of God*

When Taryn and I were at Restoring the Foundations, we learned about an unhealthy pattern of thoughts in our lives called the shame-fear-control cycle.[4] This cycle originated in the Garden of Eden. When Adam and Eve disobeyed God, the *shame* of their nakedness led them to be *fearful* of being exposed, so they took *control* and sewed fig leaves to cover themselves.

Shame can be defined as "being uniquely and hopelessly flawed."[5] Shame insidiously creeps in when we make wrong assumptions about our identity, such as my belief that I was dumb because I had difficulty reading. I felt ashamed that I couldn't read well and feared that people would discover my inadequacy, so I constantly tried to control my circumstances so people would not find out what I believed about myself. Once I recognized this destructive pattern in my life, I could expose the interconnected web of lies and break out of the shame-fear-control cycle.

I was tired of my mood being so intrinsically tied with how well I had done or how many compliments I had received, so I asked God to help me find my affirmation from Him rather than needing it from others. John 8:32 says, "Then you will know the truth, and the truth will set you free." I realized this couldn't be just something I knew intellectually. In order for me to experience the freedom this verse promises, it needed to become something I felt in my core. I asked God to show me who I was to Him. As I came across His thoughts toward me in His Word, I started meditating on His truth. The theme He repeatedly showed me was that I was His son and He was crazy about me.

I broke out of the thought pattern that I was on my own to succeed in life and that God's acceptance of me was conditional. I asked God to help me identify anyone that I needed to forgive for reinforcing this lie in my life. After I forgave each person, I intentionally exchanged this ungodly belief for the new godly belief God spoke over me: *I am a loved son of God. I have everything I need to fulfill His plan for my life.*

I found Scriptures that support this truth, such as 1 John 3:1: "See what great love the Father has lavished on us, that we should be called children of God! And that is what we are!" Another verse I frequently meditate on is 1 Peter 2:9: "But you are a chosen people, a royal priesthood, a holy nation, God's special possession, that you may declare the praises of him who called you out of darkness into his wonderful light." These verses have been helpful for me, and I meditate on them and keep them in sight to reinforce these truths in my life. As you continue to read and study the Bible, He'll highlight specific verses that will help you in just the way you need.

How has your life been affected by the performance trap? What circumstances in your life have wounded you, opening the door to lies that have influenced your relationship with God or others or caused you to adjust your actions to gain the approval of others? What activities or actions have you used to cover up your shame or avoid being exposed?

I suggest that you talk with someone if the performance trap and the shame-fear-control cycle have been a part of your life. I recommend a pastor, a Christian counselor, or your Whole Life partner—someone whom you trust and feel comfortable talking with about the trigger points that cause you to perform for love. Something powerful happens when you talk it through with another person. Be encouraged! This trap affected me and my relationships for years and years, but I have found freedom, and you can, too.

UNGODLY BELIEF #2: The "Fear of Man" Trap

Another unhealthy thought pattern that many of us fall into is the "fear of man" trap. This fear is closely connected to the performance trap and leads us to continually seek the approval of others. However, while the performance trap is primarily a lie rooted in a wrong understanding of God, the "fear of man" trap is a lie rooted in a wrong belief about ourselves. For many years of my life, I thought I needed everyone to like me at all times, and when I felt that they didn't, my inner world became a mess. I inadvertently started correlating my worth not only with my performance but also with how much I felt others approved of me.

This ungodly belief causes you to be overly concerned with what others think of you. Perhaps you were the kid who was always chosen last for kickball or never invited to the sleepovers at your friends' houses. The rejection hurt deeply and made you believe that others were out to get you and would always hurt you. Fortunately, you survived into adulthood, but you still find yourself in a similar situation when you are overlooked for a promotion at work or turned down for a date. The rejection hits a nerve deep within in your soul, fueled by the memories of earlier years. As for me, I hated any type of rejection.

It was during Taryn's and my time at Restoring the Foundations that I discovered after reflection that I had been working very hard to steer clear of rejection as much as possible by unintentionally rejecting others or distancing myself from them before they rejected me.

Our desire for approval inevitably places an unhealthy burden on our relationships. When we aren't sure how someone feels about us, we will automatically distance ourselves from them, assuming the worst. This can quickly become a downward spiral. Often what we interpret as a negative reaction may be something as simple as the other party being preoccupied by their own day-to-day happenings. Our false beliefs that others don't like us often lead us to distance ourselves from them, in turn causing others to distance themselves further from us. It's a vicious cycle but one we can break when we stop seeking approval from other people and start seeking approval from the Almighty.

SOLUTION #2: *Living for God's Approval*

Proverbs 29:25 says, "Fear of man will prove to be a snare, but whoever trusts in the Lord is kept safe." Seeking to be free from the trap of placing too much importance on what others think is a process of learning to replace the fear of man with trust in God. We can learn that it is ungodly to seek approval from others but still struggle to let God's unconditional love for us pervade our thoughts. When we recognize the ungodly belief that people will reject us if they really know who we are, we must first reject it. Here are some specific points that I encourage you to pray through to reset yourself:

1. Father, I ask You to forgive me for living for the approval of others, and I receive Your forgiveness.

2. On the basis of Your forgiveness, Lord, I choose to forgive myself for living for the approval of others.

3. I renounce every resulting curse that comes with living for the approval of others from my life through the redemptive work of Christ on the cross.

4. Father, I receive Your freedom from living for the approval of others and I now refocus my soul on pleasing my Father in heaven.

5. I ask for your help to live for You alone, in Jesus' Name, Amen.

After you have rejected this ungodly belief, ask God to replace it with a new thought. The new godly belief God gave me to focus on was that *He accepts me for who I am and who He created me to be. Therefore, I can take off the mask.* This is closely tied to the godly belief that we are beloved children of God. I realized that if I am not living with a true understanding of who I am to God, I place an unnecessary burden on my relationships. Some scriptures that reinforced my new belief were Ephesians 2:10, "We are God's handiwork, created in Christ Jesus to do good works"; and Zephaniah 3:17, "He will take great delight in you; in his love he will no longer rebuke you, but will rejoice over you with singing," both powerful replacements for the lies I previously believed.

One thing that I love about God is that He reveals in our lives that which *He wants to heal.* He doesn't just show us our issues and leave us stuck there. He empowers us through His Holy Spirit to enact real change in our lives. I have found that transparency begets transparency: When we confess our weaknesses, those weaknesses become a catalyst for others to share their wounds and fears. James 5:16 instructs us to "confess your sins to each other and pray for each other so that you may be healed." Confession leads to healing and reminds us of the role we are meant to play in each other's freedom.

When we are firmly rooted in God's acceptance, it is easier to risk sharing our authentic self in relationships because people's opinions of us don't define us—God's opinion does. The ironic part is that when we expose our insecurities and the parts of ourselves we would rather hide from those we are closest to, we are typically met with acceptance, the opposite of rejection. Sharing our vulnerabilities most often creates an atmosphere of trust and strengthens the relationship. This leads to a healthy belief-expectation-experience cycle (more on this later), where we expect to be met with grace and unconditional love, which in turn leads us to share more of ourselves and experience more connection.

UNGODLY BELIEF #3: The Broken Relationship Trap

There has been no relationship more negatively affected by my struggle with the performance and "fear of man" traps than my marriage. Taryn also struggled with these same two traps in her life, although they manifested in different ways. We had significant challenges communicating with and understanding each other, a situation that was only exacerbated by our individual brokenness and ungodly beliefs. Although Taryn and I have always loved each other very much, we had some unhealthy patterns that led to distance in our marriage and a lot of unintentional hurt.

Taryn and I had a really rough first year of marriage. By the time of our retreat, after several years of marriage, we learned that the damage done in the first year was repeating itself over and over again in our lives. Our counselor taught us about relational love maps, which explain how certain patterns in your relationship become hardwired in your brain and affect how you see the rest of your relationship, like a negative filter. In our first year of marriage, our negative patterns formed clouded lenses through which we saw each other. We discovered that these lenses actually turned into ungodly beliefs about each other and affected almost all of our interactions. The main ungodly belief that all others stemmed from was *My wife and I will never be able to have a healthy marriage and family.*

In my marriage, I erroneously viewed Taryn as irresponsible and untrustworthy in completing basic tasks I asked her to do. In our first year of marriage, there were numerous occasions where it seemed like she wouldn't complete a simple task we had both agreed she would finish. It could be something like picking out our next vacation destination, selecting a paint color for our house, or choosing a restaurant for date night. When it came time to share her decision, she typically didn't have an answer. Over time, I would get frustrated and angry; I felt disrespected by her because, in my mind, she was not valuing or prioritizing the making of decisions. We got stuck in the belief-expectation-experience cycle, and I ultimately stopped asking her for help with many decisions because I both viewed her through the lens of irresponsibility and expected her to drop the ball. This, of course, led us to both feel isolated from each other, and we continued in this unhealthy pattern for many years.

We discovered that I was not the only one with a negative lens. Taryn realized she was viewing me through the lens of incompetence in the area of household chores. Early in our marriage, whenever I tried to help with a chore like unloading the dishwasher or cleaning the kitchen, she made it clear to me that what I had done was not up to her standard. My goal was to just get it done; quality cleaning was optional. I remember the disappointment she expressed when I went to a grocery store to get her list of requested items and came home with one wrong item. She was mad I missed one item (performance), and I got angry because she didn't say thank you (fear of man). Taryn's thought was: *Why is it so hard for David to follow simple instructions? He's not taking my requests seriously.* I felt like she was being too critical and too hard to please.

After this, I pretty much stopped helping with all kitchen chores. This seemed to work pretty well for us—until we had kids. All of a sudden, there was more housework than Taryn could handle, but she still viewed me through the lens of not being able to live up to her standard for how basic chores were done. I avoided most household chores, including many of the daily tasks for the kids. After all, I did not want to do things that drew criticism. For the first several years after founding D.C. Metro, I began to stay at church later, not only because of the heavy load I was carrying at work, but also because I was subconsciously avoiding my home life. This created a growing frustration and resentment within Taryn and made her feel alone in caring for our children.

We both felt incredibly stuck in these patterns and didn't know how to escape. We also had no idea that in all areas of discord in our marriage, we were functioning from a place of past hurts that resulted in ungodly beliefs about each other because of the truth behind the belief-experience-expectation cycle. We knew that God had more in mind for our marriage, but we didn't know how to find it.

SOLUTION #3: *Breaking the Cycle*

What Taryn and I didn't realize at the time was how our own ungodly beliefs and brokenness were at play. We each had significant blind spots. Taryn realized that her indecisiveness stemmed from a deep fear of making the wrong choice, leading her to postpone even the most basic decisions. She wanted more time to evaluate and weigh out all the options so that she could choose the perfect option.

While we were in counseling, she began to connect the dots and uncovered her ungodly belief of perfectionism. She also feared disappointing me with a decision, which was rooted in her own fear of man. These revelations shattered my own incorrect view of her as irresponsible and helped me feel much more supportive of her. Now when we make decisions I ensure that she has all the necessary information up front, give her an adequate amount of time to think things over, and, above all, reassure her that every decision doesn't have to be perfect. This not only has deepened my love for Taryn but healed years of hurt. Currently, Taryn is planning a vacation for the family, and has been doing this for years now as a practice to get better at this area. I feel like I have so much grace and love for her that I have zero requirements and ultimately don't even mind if our vacation never happens. I love that she is attempting to grow in an area that is a challenge to her, and I am able to sit on the sidelines and cheer her on.

In my battle with fear of man, I tried to avoid Taryn. When there were household chores to do, I stayed late at work. I felt that no matter how hard I tried, I couldn't please her. When I shared my feelings with her, she recognized the faulty lens through which she was seeing me. She understood that I was willing to help her but that she needed to alleviate the pressure that she was unknowingly placing on me to do all my household chores perfectly.

After Taryn understood what was happening, almost immediately I began to get authentic affirmation after completing the simplest of tasks. I found that affirmation was now coming from the home more than from the office, resulting in me leaving the office earlier!

To our incredible surprise, as we resolved individual struggles, we have also created a healthier dynamic and rhythm in our marriage. We choose to expect the best of each other and communicate more openly. We are careful not to view each other through our old lenses and deliberately meditate on our godly beliefs. As we do, the old lies are removed and a deeper connection is established. As part of our new patterns, we walk, weather permitting, and pray together every night for about thirty minutes. This usually consists of fifteen minutes of chitchat regarding the day and fifteen minutes praying for each other and the needs of our friends and family. We are both incredibly thankful, as this was the desire of both of our hearts all along. We credit the renewal of our marriage with the godly belief that we both focus on: *God is giving us a healthy and whole marriage that will be an inspiration to millions.*

A RENEWED MIND FOR YOURSELF

Romans 12:2 says, "Do not conform to the pattern of this world," pointing out that the world's pattern of thinking is different from God's pattern of thinking. The verse goes on to state: "Be transformed by the renewing of your mind." The opportunity to partner with God to renew your minds is a gift He offers to all believers. The result of a renewed mind is that you *will* find the good, pleasing, and perfect will of God. But in order to attain this, we've got to understand the two patterns at battle: the one of this world and the one of God.

The Pattern of the World

The world's pattern of thinking starts with a thought that is not from God. It might be a simple thought about a circumstance where you don't have all the facts. Your husband has been coming home late all week, and you wonder if he's really been at the office. Your boss was not happy with your last project, and you begin to think that your job isn't secure. If the origin of the thought is not questioned, it begins to swirl around in the mind and can run wild: *My marriage is headed toward divorce*, or *I'm about to be fired from my job.*

Uncontrolled thoughts that run wild without a reality check can ultimately allow ungodly beliefs about ourselves and God to influence our state of mind. When we agree with the enemy's thoughts, we end up making decisions that take us far from what God desires for us. And when we start making decisions based on fallacies we often get trapped in this way of thinking. Soon enough, we start basing our entire identities on thoughts and beliefs that aren't even true.

The dangerous thing is that we have untrue thoughts *every day*. The enemy wants to entice us to question our identities by placing these thoughts in our minds. If we aren't vigilant about comparing our thoughts to Scripture, these untruths can run wild in our lives and will eventually destroy us.

Let's look at the scenario of your husband coming home late all week. Questioning a spouse's motives or whereabouts often stems from insecurity in past relationships. Because of previous scenarios encountered, she immediately wonders if he's been in an accident or worse when he doesn't come home on time the first night. Of course, she is relieved when he finally arrives. But after two or three nights of coming home late, she starts to conjure images of another woman.

I heard a story recently about a seminary student who would regularly study late at the campus library. One day his wife was informed by a nosy neighbor that the library was closed during the hours he was supposedly studying. Her thoughts might have run wild based on this information. Fortunately, the wife knew that there were two libraries on campus.

There is a healthy fear that keeps us from doing foolish things, like driving in an ice storm or letting our kids play at a house where someone has the flu. But an unhealthy fear is based on something that has not happened and may never happen. When thoughts from the enemy take root in our minds, we may panic only because we see others panicking, and in turn we spread the same sense of unfounded fear and panic to others.

When we agree with thoughts from the enemy, fear enters. Fear is a favorite tactic of the enemy to get us to question the truth. Our God is for us, not against us. (See Romans 8:31.) When fear enters into our minds, we start adjusting our actions. The enemy wants to cause confusion, panic, and chaos in our lives to blot out the peace of God.

The world's pattern of thinking is a powerful force that can affect every area of our lives, impairing our ability to live a whole life. God does not intend for our lives to be ruled by the pattern of the world. He has a way for us to replace the enemy's thoughts with His thoughts.

God's Simple Solution

The enemy has a plan for your thinking—and it's not a plan that's in your favor. But God has a better plan, and it's always to our benefit.

Second Corinthians 10:3–5 says, "For though we live in the world, we do not wage war as the world does. The weapons we fight with are not the weapons of the world. On the contrary, they have divine power to demolish strongholds. We demolish arguments and every pretension that sets itself up against the knowledge of God, and we take captive every thought to make it obedient to Christ."

To destroy or demolish a stronghold means to tear it, break it, rip it—do whatever it takes to make it die. Our hope is to replace it with a brand-new pattern of thinking to live by. This is exciting, because we always have the choice of a better option. We don't ever have to conform to the pattern of the world and instead can transform through the renewal of our minds.

The enemy wants to steer your thinking in a direction that will leave you ensnared and in trouble in all areas of your life. When we take our thoughts captive and hand them over to God, the enemy no longer has power over us. To hold a thought captive, instead of worrying over it, we stop, rethink our options, and decide that God is bigger than whatever we are dealing with. *My God is able to do immeasurably more than whatever power I believe this circumstance holds.* In fact, "I can do all things through Him who strengthens me" (Philippians 4:13).[6] Once we do this, we begin to realize the true power of God's Word.

In Philippians 4:8, Paul tells us the thoughts we are to have: "Finally, brothers and sisters, whatever is true, whatever is noble, whatever is right, whatever is pure, whatever is lovely, whatever is admirable—if anything is excellent or praiseworthy—think about such things." Whenever you start to feel troubled, chances are you're meditating on falsehoods. When this happens, identify the lies and turn your thoughts toward the truth and power that comes from the Word of God.

If your circumstances don't look promising, remember that there is a difference between fact and truth. A fact is how things are. The truth is who God is. And truth always trumps fact no matter what is happening. Another version of Philippians 4:8 says "let your mind dwell on these things."[7] I like the word *dwell* because it communicates staying put and lingering. Keep your thoughts on the truth of the Word of God, continuing to return to what He says is good over and over.

To keep my thoughts focused on God's Word, I bring Romans 8:31 to mind as often as I need, personalizing it to my circumstances: If God is for *me*, then who can be against *me*? I then imagine what amazing things God will do in my situation and throughout my day. As I do this, I replace my ungodly beliefs with godly beliefs and am empowered to look at my circumstances through a lens of hope. If God got me through my last problem, I have faith that He is going to get me through the next one, too. His imagination is bigger than mine, so I am free to dream and partner with Him in the next solution. As you start to agree with the truth of God, His faithfulness becomes evident based on that truth in your life.

It is imperative to have this mind-set as we walk in the clarified dream I talked about in chapter four. As we saw in the promise-problem-provision cycle, obstacles most definitely will come when we are pursuing God's dream and purpose for our lives. The lens through which we view those problems, and how we choose to react to them, is a significant factor in whether or not our clarified dream becomes a reality.

When you believe in the truth God provides, your thought patterns naturally change. There is a whole field of study called cognitive behavioral therapy that focuses on this concept. This model reflects the belief that psychological disorders develop through distorted thinking, and the symptoms associated with such disorders can be *reduced* by teaching new information-processing skills."[8]

Whenever you practice new godly beliefs, you are teaching yourself new information and turning it into a skill. Your godly beliefs eventually become so rooted that a new, godly thought pattern becomes second nature, which allows the Spirit to free you from the tether of these destructive thoughts. Depending on what you agree with, whether a lie or the truth, the result will always remain: Lies lead to strongholds, but God's truth leads to freedom in your life!

A BEAUTIFUL MIND

God designed you with an identity as His son or daughter. That means you can go to Him anytime, day or night, and tell Him your troubles. When you ask God to help change your earthly situation, believe and be ready to change your ungodly beliefs into new and inspirational godly beliefs that He already believes about you. He will be faithful to do it—but first you have to ask and believe. Even after you receive your new godly beliefs, as we will discuss in the next section, you must remain on guard. The enemy often tries to use our season of waiting to instill doubt. As soon as your thoughts start to run wild with what-ifs or unbelief, turn away and replace them with God thoughts. This sets in motion a new pattern in your life that will result in freedom and ultimate victory. God has created you with a beautiful mind, but it's up to you to keep it beautiful. Below are the seven steps involved in discovering and changing ungodly beliefs.

1. Identify Any Ungodly Beliefs

Ungodly beliefs are often buried underneath our "Sunday school" answers about who God is. We can articulate correct theology that God is faithful and that He will provide for us, but we may still have hidden ungodly beliefs underneath the surface telling us He won't. Only when we take a deep and honest look at ourselves can we replace our unbelief with God's truth.

Review the list of common ungodly beliefs I shared earlier in this chapter to help you identify which ones you might be holding. You can also ask God to reveal any ungodly beliefs or thoughts about Him, yourself, or others that do not line up with His Word. David prayed in Psalm 139:23, "Search me, God, and know my heart; test me and know my anxious thoughts."

2. Reject Agreement with the Ungodly Belief

The next step is to confess and ask God to forgive you for the partnership you've made with the enemy's lies, and tell Him you're ready to break your agreement with them. Ask Him to reveal anyone who has instilled or contributed to the lies, and forgive whomever He brings to mind.

3. Ask God for a Godly Belief

Once you have rejected your ungodly belief, ask God to speak a specific truth to counteract the lie. I encourage you to pause and listen to see if you hear Him say anything specific. It is natural to want to automatically write down the opposite of the ungodly belief, but the most powerful godly beliefs are ones that you hear God speak directly to you. If you do not hear or sense anything specific, you can look to Scripture or write what you know to be true.

For example, if your ungodly belief was *Relationships are more trouble than they are worth, and I don't need to be in relationship with others,* then your godly belief might be *God has specific relationships for me that will help me grow and develop into the person whom He is calling me to be.* I call this the divine exchange. Anytime we lay down something before Him, God always wants to replace it with something better.

4. Look Up Scriptures to Reinforce Your Godly Beliefs

I typically try to find several scriptures for each new godly belief. As previously mentioned, concordances exist where you can look up scriptures topically. You can also do a topical Google search or go to Bible Gateway for scriptures relating to the truth you're looking for. For the godly belief *God has specific relationships for me that will help me grow and develop into who He is calling me to be,* you could look up scriptures about relationships or friendship.

Proverbs 27:17 is a perfect example: "As iron sharpens iron, so a friend sharpens a friend."[9] Ecclesiastes 4:9–12 is also a great choice: "Two are better than one, because they have a good return for their labor: If either of them falls down, one can help the other up. But pity anyone who falls and has no one to help them up. Also, if two lie down together, they will keep warm. But how can one keep warm alone? Though one may be overpowered, two can defend themselves. A cord of three strands is not quickly broken."

5. Write Your Three Godly Beliefs and Supporting Scriptures

For the next step, I encourage you to write down your new godly beliefs and the scriptures that reinforce this truth on an index card or a sticky note. Place them somewhere you'll see them frequently, like your bathroom mirror or the dashboard of your car. I have a friend who sets a reminder on his phone and has these encouraging verses and beliefs pop up at a certain time each day so he is forced to read them. For my example, I would write down my godly belief *God has specific relationships for me that will help me grow and develop into who He is calling me to be* and the two scriptures I mentioned above that support that belief.

6. Meditate on These Truths

Next, as we read and meditate on God's truths, our minds are actually being renewed. I encourage you to meditate on your godly beliefs and scriptures every day for thirty days. After thirty days, if you feel like you haven't internalized the truths yet, I urge you to keep meditating on them for another thirty days. Even after you believe the godly belief has taken root in your life, it is good to review these truths at least once a week to keep them fresh in your mind and be on guard against the enemy's attacks.

7. Take Thoughts Captive

Finally, as 2 Corinthians 10:5 says, we are to take our thoughts captive and make them obedient to Christ. We must be ready for any thoughts that come into our minds that align with our ungodly belief or old patterns of thinking. We have to be diligent to recognize and reject these; they can subtly creep back in if we are not careful.

For example, if you start to have negative thoughts about yourself, it's easy to partner with the thought when that is what you're used to doing. Instead, God calls you to be vigilant about claiming the truth of what He says about you. My three-year-old daughter, Karis, boldly approaches new people and introduces herself with "Hello, my name is Karis, and I am Daddy's princess." I believe God wants us to have that same confidence in our identity as a loved son or daughter of the Father. As you meditate on your godly beliefs and scriptures, and as you proactively take your thoughts captive, I believe you will begin living out the promise in 1 Corinthians 2:16 and cultivate a Christlike mind.

REVIEW

Our thoughts affect our actions, which in turn determine if we walk in our God-given dream. In this chapter I introduced ungodly beliefs: thoughts, attitudes, and ideas that do not line up with God's will and purposes for us. Drawing from my personal experience, I gave details about three specific ungodly beliefs—the performance trap, the fear-of-man trap, and the broken relationship trap—and the solutions we found to address those beliefs. I also talked about a maintenance measure that Taryn and I have taken to protect our Whole Life marriage of walking and praying together each night.

I talked about the need for us to realign our minds with God's pattern instead of that of the world and outlined a seven-step process to cultivate a Christlike mind: identifying ungodly beliefs, rejecting agreement with those ungodly beliefs, asking God for a godly belief, finding scriptures to reinforce our godly belief, writing down our godly beliefs and supporting scriptures, meditating on His truths, and taking our thoughts captive.

WHOLE LIFE CHALLENGE

Your first challenge for this chapter is found within the chapter. If you have not already done so, I encourage you to review the list of ungodly beliefs and walk through the subsequent steps under the subheading "A Beautiful Mind." As you create your own positive declarations and recite them daily, you will undo the negative declarations you have spoken or meditated on in the past. I recommend that you come up with at least three godly beliefs that you can write down and begin to commit to memory as declarations over your life.

As an additional challenge, commit to reciting these out loud every morning for the next six weeks by putting them on an index card and placing them on your bathroom mirror. By verbally reciting these declarations over your life during the next six weeks, you will find a renewed confidence as a son or daughter of God and a restored faith to see them become evident in your daily life. You will also find yourself taking large strides toward having a transformed mind that is able to easily fight off the patterns of this world as you walk in wholeness.

Will

six

Will—It's Your Choice

*The world is full of willing people, some willing
to work, the rest willing to let them.*
—Robert Frost

*My food, said Jesus, "is to do the will of Him
who sent me and to finish His work."*
—John 4:34

In the Garden of Eden, God gave Adam and Eve a choice; they could eat from all the trees in the garden—including the Tree of Life—but not from the tree of the knowledge of good and evil. The significance of this choice—to obey or disobey God—was great: spiritual life or death. We all know the end of the story: they made the wrong choice and ate from the one tree that God told them to avoid.

Adam and Eve's ability to choose between the trees illustrates that God gave humans free will. As the second component to Soul Care, we will focus on aligning our will—the part of our soul that makes decisions—with that of God. We make thousands of decisions each day—some major, like who to marry or where to work, and some minor, like what to wear or what to eat for breakfast.

It is the human will that decides between good and bad, right and wrong. God did not create Adam and Eve to be like robots, prepro-grammed to act a certain way, to fulfill a certain purpose, to obey Him, or even to make right choices. God has purpose for our lives. He also has given us wisdom and direction in the Bible to help us decide what He desires for us, but He leaves the ultimate choice to us. Joshua

24:15 states: "Choose for yourselves this day whom you will serve." Clearly, God has a will that He desires us to be a part of, but we have a human will that makes the choice to serve Him daily or to ignore Him.

The choice between the two trees in the garden was the first expression of how God designed man with a human will. It is also the first time that the human will was in conflict with God's will. Which brings up the question: Who is in charge? If I have a will that is free to choose, but God is somehow in charge of everything and has a will for my life, how do He and I work together to get me to my dream and purpose in this life?

God's Will or Ours?

There was a great movie that came out in 2011 called *The Adjustment Bureau*. The story revolves around the employees of the Adjustment Bureau, whose job is to ensure that humans follow "the plan" of the bureau's chairman. The bureau employees—angel types—carry tablets that have a sort of GPS on them, directing humans on their set path. The main character, David Norris, deviates from the plan for his life when he falls in love with a woman, Elise, he meets in passing.

The bureau employees try to keep David away from Elise, finally revealing themselves to David to tell him he is messing up the chairman's plan for his life, to become the president of the United States. David doesn't care about his future, only wanting the woman of his dreams. The final scene is of David and Elise standing on the observation deck of the GE building, being interrupted by a bureau employee who shows them a revised plan from the chairman: He can still become president and have the relationship with Elise.

God has a plan for our lives, but in allowing us the freedom to choose, there is a flexibility we experience as we search for His will. Romans 8:28 says, "We know that in all things God works for the good of those who love him, who have been called according to his purpose." For those called according to His purpose, the "all things" that work together somehow include even our wrong choices. If we love Him, He gets us to our purpose and destiny one way or another.

Remember, God is not bound by time: He sees the end from the beginning. Although we are not robots or puppets blindly following His plans, He is still sovereign over His creation and our lives. Sovereignty basically means God has the final say. For me, there is freedom and grace in the knowledge that as I make choices with my will, if I make a bad decision, the story is not necessarily over.

Finding His Will

As a believer, our will should desire to find and choose to obey His direction for our lives. In order to find God's will for your life, you're going to have to look for it! Matthew 6:33 tells us, "Seek first His kingdom and His righteousness, and all these things will be given to you as well." Seeking the Kingdom of God requires you to put God first in all areas of your life.

The phrase *His righteousness* is actually an important Greek term that directly translates to "what is deemed right by God" or His right pattern for living.[1] So we can say it like this: Seek first the Kingdom of God and *His right pattern for how to live*, and then all those "other things" will be added to you.

As we seek God's will by putting Him first, we often think the other priorities in life will naturally fall in line. Unfortunately, this is not the case. Truly putting God first includes implementing His pattern—or His priorities—for living in every area of our lives before anything else. When we are not actively doing this, we are living what I call the accidental life, placing too much priority on the "extra" things in life: social media, entertainment, sports, hobbies, shopping, and casual acquaintances. These things aren't bad, but they were never meant to be our main focus and do not lead to deep or meaningful connection with God or others.

Think of life as an empty paper bag. God has given us this paper bag clean, with so many possibilities, but there are only a certain number of things that will fit into our lives. Each life has its limitations, and, like the bag, we can't always fit in everything we desire. When the different elements of our lives are not placed in the right order, we end up with a life filled with the insignificant. By not living according to God's priorities, we end up with a life bursting at the seams as we try to fit more and more in.

In this analogy, I like to use sand to represent all those extras, or nonessential activities, that lead to an accidental life. If you pour sand into your bag first, all the other larger elements—God, family, career—stick out of the bag, and your bag soon topples over. Through this illustration, we quickly see what an out-of-balance life looks like. But when you put God (represented by a pocket Bible) first, family (represented by toy figures for spouse and children) second, Christian community (represented by a coffee cup) third, and work (represented by a smartphone) fourth, you can fit all the items—and then some—in the bag. When we wait to pour the sand "extras" over the items of our lives last, we can see how full and meaningful our lives become when we align our choices with God's priorities. This fullness comes from having everything in the right order. When our lives are balanced and properly prioritized, our bag does not risk ripping or tipping over from too many demands.

This illustration simply but powerfully helps us to see how critical it is to choose God's priorities as our priorities. When the elements of our lives are out of order, we can often feel overwhelmed and burned-out because nothing is fitting together the way it's supposed to. But when our lives follow God's order, we experience something completely different: a significant and fulfilling life.

After I started processing this concept, I began to make some challenging but important shifts in my own life to rediscover His rhythm. Whenever we realize we are out of rhythm and our priorities are off, it is incredibly important not only to ask what we need to shift but what we need to change in our thoughts and habits to facilitate this shift.

In realigning our lives to fit with God's priorities, it's critical to perform a constant personal inventory and question the motives behind our daily activities and decisions. This is often more difficult than it seems. If you're overworked and neglecting your family, it might be because you fear failing in your career, or you might be trying to avoid unresolved problems in your marriage that rear their heads when you are home. After taking a close look at our lives, we need to take authority over our ungodly thoughts and replace them with God's truth. Once your mind is in alignment with His truth, your will naturally follows suit, leading you out of an accidental life and back into one of God's purpose and plan.

In order to lead a life of significance, we need to be discerning about what takes up our time. Intentionality in all life's decisions leads to a life in accordance with God's will and steers us away from the accidental life. As Christians, we have to realize that every time we say yes to something, we are saying no to something else. If we don't do this with diligence, we'll conform to the pattern and priorities of the world and individuals around us.

Say Yes to God's Priorities

Priorities are like a hardwired set of decisions that we make subconsciously. That's why it's important to revisit what God's priorities for us are. Over time, our priorities can get out of alignment based on the pressures of life—requiring an adjustment to get back in line with God's will. It is kind of like going to the chiropractor for your will.

So, what are God's priorities, and what order should they fit into our lives as we choose to seek His will? The answer to this is seen in Matthew 6:33, "Seek first His kingdom and His righteousness . . ." This is the first and foremost priority for every one of us. When we are faithful in seeking His will and His right path, He will add all the other things needed in our lives in a way that will work together in harmony.

Our lives are not formulas where you input your responsibilities into an equation of priorities and come out with the right answer. Instead, God calls us to be in relationship with Him and to listen for His still, small voice when it comes time to make decisions. The order of our priorities also doesn't determine how much time we're to spend on each area. Rather than an exact correlation of time spent in our schedules, I believe this order is more about the priority each of these areas should have in our hearts and can be used to help us when making important decisions in life.

I have found the only way I can truly know what to choose and when to choose it is to listen to God by spending time in prayer, studying the Bible, and hearing His direction through others. (Discover more about this topic in my book, *Hearing from God.*) When we do, we are allowing His Spirit to lead our spirits. When our spirits are in alignment with His, our thoughts become like His, and we are able to make decisions in line with His will. I believe that as you seek Him, He will show you what prioritizing looks like in your schedule.

Ultimately, the best process is to make the realignment based on God's priorities and then review the new list of life's priorities until it becomes second nature. A good place to put your new set of life priorities is wherever you keep your calendar. Since the things that make your calendar are premeditated decisions, having this list handy when you set your calendar can be very helpful.

Let's look at God's priorities in order of importance so that you can assess and realign your priorities.

PRIORITY ONE: *God Himself*

The first Whole Life priority is found in Luke 10:27, where Jesus instructs us to "love the Lord your God with all your heart and with all your soul and with all your strength and with all your mind." Your heart is typically thought to be the core of who you are; your soul is your mind, will, and emotions; and your strength comes from your physical body. It is interesting to note that He includes the mind at the end. Whenever Jesus repeats Himself in Scripture, I know I should pay really close attention. In this passage, Jesus is calling on us to love God with our whole beings: spirit, soul, and body, not with just part of who we are, which is what I was trying to do before God spoke to me through 1 Thessalonians 5:23. This is why I believe that focusing on finding and maintaining rhythm in our Whole Life is a significant aspect of priority number one.

I encourage you to evaluate any area of your life where God is not first. When I am assessing my life for idols (things I've given a higher priority than God), I ask myself where I run when I am in need of comfort or pleasure. What is taking up the most mental real estate in my mind? I ask God to show me if there is anything or anyone I love more than Him.

PRIORITY TWO: Family

If you are married, your family—spouse and children—should be the second priority on your list. In Ephesians 5 we see God's desired relationship between a husband and wife. Women are called to respect their husbands, and husbands are instructed to "love your wives, just as Christ loved the church and gave himself up for her" (Ephesians 5:25). We should prioritize our spouse in the same way Christ prioritized His church. First Timothy 3:5 talks about the importance of family when it says, "If anyone does not know how to manage his own family, how can he take care of God's church?" Your first ministry, before we even talk about other ministries, should be your family.

If you are single, I encourage you to focus on your family of origin and close friendships. When your family of origin is not in the picture or not supportive of you, God desires you to have friendships that become like family. These are relationships where you find companionship and emotional support through life's ups and downs, people you trust and are comfortable with. Whether you are eventually called to marriage, or your call is to the single life, live this season to its fullest.

PRIORITY THREE: *Church/God-First Relationships*

Priority three is connecting in a local community of believers. Psalm 92:13 says those who are planted in God's house will flourish. Hebrews 10:24–25 says, "Let us consider how we may spur one another on toward love and good deeds, not giving up meeting together, as some are in the habit of doing, but encouraging one another—and all the more as you see the Day approaching."

If you're not involved in a local body of believers, then you are missing out on an important part of God's plan for your life. Not only do you need a church family, they need you; you have gifts, talents, experiences, and wisdom that will benefit others who are also seeking a close community in which to worship, serve God, and share life together.

There are a few ways you can find a church home. Ask your friends where they attend, and find out what they consider to be the strengths and weaknesses of their churches. Do a Google search of the churches in your city, check out their websites, or make note of churches you drive by on your way to work or school. Make a list of what you are looking for in a church: small groups, contemporary or traditional worship, or strong outreach ministries. Compare your list of desires with what you learn about different congregations. Based on your research, make a list of which churches you want to visit. Throughout the process, ask God to show you where He wants you! He has a great home church near you. There is always room in God's house.

If you are already a regular church attender, I encourage you to meet with an elder, deacon, staff member, priest, or pastor to help you find a good place to serve. There is an amazing paradox in God's economy. When we serve in His house, we typically end up feeling like we have received more than we have given. I have always found that I am more willing to serve others on Monday when I have already served God, at His house, on Sunday. Being in a church community will allow you to develop God-first relationships, which is a huge part of God's plan for our lives. God wants us not to be isolated from each other but to be able to share our lives and learn from one another. Your closest relationships don't necessarily have to all be friendships from your church, but I think church is one of the best places to find, develop, and grow friendships. Many churches have small groups or Bible studies to encourage development of close friendships that can last you through life, support you, and hold you accountable.

Paul wrote to the church in Corinth in 2 Corinthians 8:5 about this type of God-first relationship. He said, "They gave themselves first of all to the Lord, and then by the will of God also to us." Notice the order in this passage says, "first of all to the Lord," but follows with "and then by *the will of God* also to us." A relationship with other believers is part of the will of God for our lives.

PRIORITY FOUR: *Work*

A fourth and critical priority is your work. This is one that some of us love and others wish we could somehow wipe off the list. The most important aspect of our work is not what we do but how we do it. Colossians 3:23 encourages us, "Whatever you do, work at it with all your heart, as working for the Lord, not for human masters." The Message translation of this verse further unpacks how we live out this verse: *Don't just do the minimum that will get you by. Do your best. Work from the heart for your real Master, for God, confident that you'll get paid in full when you come into your eternal inheritance. Keep in mind always that the ultimate Master you're serving is Christ.*

I believe your work is meant to be your ministry. You may be involved in a ministry at church or in the community, but I challenge you to see the place where you spend the majority of your week as a central aspect of your ministry. Ephesians 2:10 says, "We are God's handiwork, created in Christ Jesus to do good works, which God prepared in advance for us to do." For everyone who has decided to follow Jesus, God turns around and says, "I have a plan for you to help Me with My plan." I don't know about you, but this thought gets me excited!

Wherever you work, there are many ways God can use you. Maybe it is in a more overtly evangelistic role where you share your walk with God with your coworkers; maybe you'll feel inspired to invite colleagues to join you for a church service. Maybe it's in subtler ways, where you do your job with such excellence and character that your boss and coworkers take notice. Proverbs 18:16 says, "A gift opens the way and ushers the giver into the presence of the great." When we work with integrity and diligence, and use the gifts God has given us in our workplaces, it opens up opportunities for glorifying Him.

God will help you steward your influence and help you recognize how you can use favor with man for His bigger purpose. If you are a stay-at-home parent or a student, or serve in a behind-the-scenes role, it can be hard to see the immediate impact you are making or how your hard work is building the Kingdom of God. I believe if you work as though you're working for the Lord in the sphere that He has called you, you are exactly where you need to be. Rest assured, God is pleased with you and will bring fruit in His way and His time. If you are faithful where He has called, you can trust He will position you to be ready to step toward your purpose when the time is right.

I encourage you to honestly assess yourself to see if you have the tendency to underperform and act like you're not working for God. Signs of underperformance include cutting corners and doing the minimum expected of you. When you work for God, you work with integrity, doing what is required for the job and more if needed. At the end of the day, you know you will answer to God for all your hard work.

Or do you fall into the other extreme of overworking and being out of sync with God's priorities? If your identity and sense of self-worth is primarily in your work, or you are looking to the job to fill up the void in your life that God wants to fill, being a workaholic will only lead you down the road to burnout! Wherever you find yourself, surrender your work life to God, remembering that He wants you to work hard but to put Him before your career.

PRIORITY FIVE: *Everything Else*

Fifth on the list is everything else I talked about earlier—all the other fun stuff we do. I've had certain seasons where I was working over seventy hours a week and had no hobbies. One of my mentors challenged me to find a hobby to serve as a healthy outlet to help me disconnect from the pressures of my responsibilities. Several years ago I took up fishing, which has become an incredible blessing in my life. It's the introvert's perfect sport, where one can be surrounded by God's incredible creation and let the stresses of the world melt away. It has also become a way for me to bond with my sons, who now share my love of fishing. We are always praying for the next "big one" and enjoy competing with each other to see who is going to reel in the largest fish in the Stine household. I also started playing tennis again. After almost twenty years away, I rediscovered my love for the game. I'm not quite the competitive player that I once was, but my priority is different now, and I use it both as a hobby and as a way to get in some great exercise. Tennis has also helped me with priority number two, my wife and my children. We all play together, and it has become a family activity, something we all love to do together to decompress and bond.

The more that you can use your "everything else" to advance the other, more important priorities, the better and more enjoyable they become as you journey toward your Whole Life rhythm. I think the extra activities in our lives can be amazing gifts that allow us to experience the goodness of God in new ways. As we seek Him, all these other things will be given to us as well in the right order and timing.

For everyone who has experienced living an accidental life, know that God gives us grace to refigure our priorities so that we can fully live in what He has called us to. The enemy has a plan for your life, and that is to steal, kill, and destroy you (see John 10:10): He wants your life out of balance and full of stress. When you are intentional about keeping your priorities in line with God's priorities, Satan's attempts become less effective and we become more able to live the abundant life that Jesus desires for each of us.

In every season of your life, as you pursue the dreams God has placed in your heart, just remember to ask these questions: Is my will choosing to follow His will? Am I putting God first? And do I have Whole Life priorities? When you answer yes to these, you know you're on target and in line with God's will. Hold tight to these priorities, because He will do "immeasurably more than we ask or imagine, according to his power that is at work within us" (Ephesians 3:20)!

REVIEW

You were created by God with a will, the ability to make choices, which is the second component of our souls. God has a dream and purpose for your life, but He allows you the choice to search after and follow His will or to ignore it. Finding His will involves discovering His priorities for a whole life and choosing to implement those priorities into the rhythm of your life.

In this chapter I introduced God's priorities for you and me: God first, family second, church and God-first relationships third, work fourth, and everything else fifth. Through the analogy of life as a paper bag, we saw that when everything is added to our lives in God's order it all fits, including the "everything else."

In Matthew 11:28–30, Jesus says, "Come to me, all you who are weary and burdened, and I will give you rest. Take my yoke upon you and learn from me, for I am gentle and humble in heart, and you will find rest for your souls. For my yoke is easy and my burden is light." I believe this is God's promise to each of us in every season of life.

It's interesting to note that Jesus specifies rest for our souls in this passage rather than rest for our bodies. When we are living His Whole Life rhythm and choosing His priorities, He will give us rest for our mind, will, and emotions—even in the midst of problems.

When we are not in His rhythm, we feel burdened, tired, and overwhelmed. As you learn to live in a Whole Life rhythm, check in with how you're feeling on a daily and weekly basis. If you're feeling exhausted or heavy in spirit, it's often a sign that your priorities and actions are not aligning with His rhythm.

WHOLE LIFE CHALLENGE

As a challenge for this chapter, find out what your priorities are by doing a simple personal inventory. To find out how you are using your time and where a realignment needs to take place, I encourage you to do two things:

1. Make a list of what you value. This could include the priorities I listed in this chapter—time with your children, prayer, work—or anything else that consumes your thoughts and time. The most important thing is to be honest with yourself so you can compare how your priorities are currently lining up with God's.

2. Create a document in which you record everything you do during the week, summarized in thirty-minute increments.

Many times there is a disconnect between what we think we do with our time and what we actually do with it. The first time I performed this inventory for myself, I was shocked at how much TV I watched! Once you have recorded your week of activities, assess where your time was used, and determine if you are using your time according to God's priorities. Look for overlaps, areas where "everything else" actually can be useful if paired with something of a higher priority. Identify these overlaps and add them into those higher priorities.

Finally, spend some time in prayer, asking God what shifts you need to make in your schedule so your time lines up with His priorities for your life and helps you to position yourself to take steps forward in your purpose. This process is sure to make His will and your will begin to intersect through these new and ordered priorities. Matthew 6:33 tells us to "seek first His kingdom and righteousness," and leaves us with the promise that the resulting blessing will be room in our lives for the "everything else."

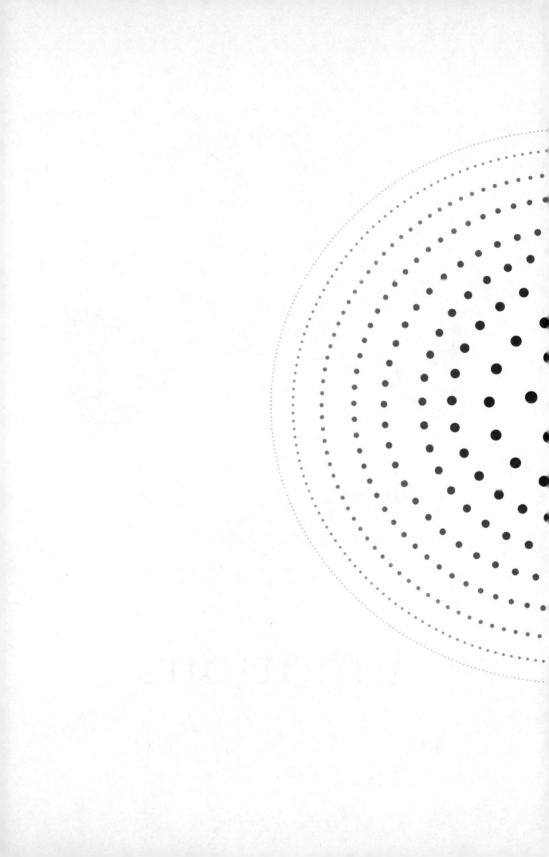

Emotions

seven

Emotions—He Restores My Soul

I don't want to be at the mercy of my emotions. I want
to use them, enjoy them, and dominate them.
—Oscar Wilde, *The Picture of Dorian Gray*

Do not forsake wisdom, and she will protect you;
love her, and she will watch over you.
The beginning of wisdom is this: Get wisdom.
Though it cost all you have, get understanding.
—King Solomon, Proverbs 4:6–7

It has been said that a picture is worth a thousand words; perhaps that is the reason that emojis are still so popular. My wife sometimes sends me a text with no less than eight cleverly placed emojis that tie into her content perfectly. One day I decided to jump on the emoji train and sent some back to her. However, I didn't have the patience to carefully select them, so I just sent her whichever ones my fingers hit first. She texted back with a confused-face emoji and asked me why I sent her a poodle in response to her question. The poodle emoji has now become a running joke between the two of us that we'll send back and forth to make each other laugh. Unprocessed emotions are similar to me randomly selecting whichever emoji my finger tapped on: They are not thought out and are sometimes irrational.

Unprocessed emotions can transform your soul into an old refrigerator that hasn't been cleaned out in a really long time. The moldy leftover Chinese takeout and the carton of sour milk make for a pretty putrid odor inside. And how about that Tupperware container hiding in the back with what looks like an amateur science experiment in it? In each of these cases, these items have been ignored past their expiration dates, and they *turned*. In a similar way, when we ignore our emotional indicators that something is wrong, our soul *turns*.

God's emotional indicators are a lot like the dashboard lights on a car that alert the driver when there is an area that needs attention: The oil level is low or the door isn't closed tight. In the same way, our mood, actions, thoughts, and words can often tell us (or others) that something in our emotional lives needs care. When our reaction to a small annoyance is overly dramatic or out of control, it's a clear sign that we are being led by our emotions rather than by our mind and will.

In my seminary counseling class, I learned that when we overreact and have a stronger emotional response than the situation warrants, it is called an emotional echo. An echo can be defined as "something that is similar to something that happened or existed before."[1] We often respond to circumstances with emotions from an unresolved past experience that don't necessarily fit or serve the current situation. For example, we might have a friendship that has gone bad. We then unconsciously search out friends who have similar personality traits like the friend with whom the relationship has gone south. In the new friendship, they may say or do something that reminds us of what happened in that unresolved relationship, and our emotional response to them is really us responding to the prior relationship—which leaves the other person feeling somewhat shocked at the unmerited level of reaction to their otherwise innocuous action.

When you come across these emotional echoes in your daily living, stop and recognize that you need help processing a past hurt. You might need to seek out professional help or the counsel of the wise friend, but, ultimately, you surrender the echo to God, asking that He heal whatever emotional imbalance exists.

AN INVERTED SOUL

Although our emotions can often baffle us, we need to remember that God created our emotions; they are good gifts from Him that help us express ourselves. In fact, Scripture reveals that God has emotions, too. He is not a passive, stoic God but One who deeply feels and lets His heart be affected by His people. The God of the Bible gets angry (2 Kings 17:18), loves (John 3:16), has loyalties (Deuteronomy 7:9), is jealous (Exodus 34:14), and feels compassion (Romans 9:15).

Because we are called to be like Jesus, we can look to His expression of emotions as our model. He was not indifferent toward His people, even in their rebellion, as we see in Luke 19:41 when He weeps over Jerusalem. But Jesus was also not ruled by His emotions, which was no more evident than when He decided to go to the cross. In Luke 22:42, His humanity is displayed in His admission that He would rather not endure the intense emotional and physical pain of crucifixion. If Jesus had let His emotions rule Him, they would not have led Him to the cross—and to our salvation.

There are two extremes when it comes to emotions. The first is when someone has cut off their ability to feel certain emotions, which typically comes from a place of self-protection. When someone has been deeply hurt in the past, they often build a wall around their heart, either knowingly or unknowingly blocking their emotions from surfacing so they won't be seen as weak or form attachments with someone who might hurt them again. When someone does this, they are actually living in fear (of getting hurt again) instead of freedom.

Whenever decisions are made from suppressed emotions, your soul's natural hierarchy is inverted; it's the reverse of God's intended order for your life. We can define an inverted soul as a will in defiance to God's will and submitted only to self and what feels right. The good news is each new day in Christ brings the opportunity for full and complete healing. You were meant to feel deeply and be able to express yourself in a healthy way, so if you feel as though you are disconnected from certain emotions, I encourage you to first talk to a trusted friend or licensed counselor.

The other extreme is when your emotions run so strong that you become controlled by them. Whenever you are governed by your feelings, you are no longer being led by the mind and Spirit of Christ. Making decisions based on how you feel means you are inadvertently saying, "My will be done." The Lord's Prayer, a prayer Jesus taught His disciples to pray, says, "Our Father in heaven, hallowed be your name, your kingdom come, your will be done, on earth as it is in heaven" (Matthew 6:9–10). We cannot allow our emotions to lead our decisions and sincerely seek to follow His will at the same time. We must choose.

When our souls become inverted from God's order and our feelings try to take charge, we need to first recognize that our soul has turned. Once we have identified that our emotions are out of balance, we can then go to God and ask Him to restore our soul. This is illustrated through Psalm 23: "The Lord is my shepherd. I shall not want. He makes me lie down in green pastures; He leads me beside quiet waters."[2] In verse three, he continues telling us what God wants to do with our inverted soul: "He restores my soul."[3] The Hebrew word translated as *restore* means to turn over or right something that is turned upside down.

Sheep can lie down and get up, but sheep oftentimes trip, fall, and flip over. In that case they lack the ability to roll over to get back on their feet; this requires the help of their shepherd. The Psalmist was very familiar with the shepherd's role in turning over inverted sheep. When a sheep is lying on its back and its feet are sticking up in the air, the sheep will soon be in big trouble. A sheep's body cannot function upside down for very long. The digestive process begins to produce gas and expands the body cavity. If left too long, it will literally squeeze the life out of the animal. When a shepherd sees an upside-down sheep, he simply goes over and flips him back to his intended position, and the sheep's life balance is restored.[4]

God does the same for us. With His help, our soul can be righted once again back to the life-giving order of mind, will, and emotions. The difference between us and the sheep is that we first have to want to be set aright. Hurt and pain are inevitable in this life, but, with Jesus, staying in that place of pain is optional. When we are hurt and don't allow God into our pain, the wall we build around our heart keeps us helpless on our backs.

After many insightful conversations with a friend who happens to be a certified Christian counselor, I have come to understand the three primary sources of most negative, painful, and hurtful emotion. Remember, all of our emotions are a part of our makeup. You can pretend as though they don't exist, but they are there. God not only wants you to talk about your emotions, He wants to help you manage each one of them, turning an inverted soul into one that's restored.

First, Allow God to Remove Your Guilt.

In my experience, there is nothing that can turn my soul over faster than guilt and all of the shame and condemnation that comes with it. King David was no stranger to the weight of guilt in his life. In Psalm 38:4, 6, he says, "My guilt has overwhelmed me like a burden too heavy to bear. . . . I am bowed down and brought very low; all day long I go about mourning." David was weighed down by guilt because his sin had led to the death of his son. When we don't deal with our guilt, it has the same effect in our lives, consuming our every thought, and leading to a sense of hopelessness and depression.

When I was a freshman in college, before I knew Jesus, experimenting with drugs and alcohol was the norm. Even though I wasn't yet living for Christ, I knew deep down that my behavior was wrong, and I felt guilty. To deal with my guilt, I decided I'd get as far away as possible from what I thought to be its source: my current group of friends. I soon heard about the National Student Exchange program, where you could pay in-state fees and go to another state's school. It was wintertime, and I like snowboarding, so I went where the mountains are really high: Utah State University. My subconscious motivation, however, was to get away from that guilt.

Not long after I arrived in Utah, I connected with the same type of friends I had left back home. They were different people with different names and faces, but they shared the same lifestyle and inspired the same bad behavior. I knew I wasn't living my life with meaningful purpose or performing up to my standards or my family's expectations. That experience taught me that even though I had left one unhealthy environment, I had failed to recognize I'd brought with me the one thing I couldn't get away from: myself. So instead of blaming others for my guilt, I began taking responsibility for my own feelings. Geographical and external adjustment can certainly facilitate inner change and healing, but the core environment that needs the most change is the heart.

HOW DO YOU DEAL WITH GUILT IN YOUR LIFE?

Proverbs 20:27 says, "The Lord gave us mind and conscience; we cannot hide from ourselves."[5] Wherever you go, you go with you. And wherever you go, your guilt goes with you as well. Simply put, your options are threefold: (1) blame others for its existence (whether the fault of the other party was intended or unintended); (2) claim responsibility yourself; or (3) acknowledge the wrong done to you and extend forgiveness to the other person.

As a pastor, I have found the most common thing people who struggle with guilt do is fall into shame and beat themselves up mentally and emotionally. When this happens, quality of life turns into negative compound interest. In other words, making decisions from a place of guilt and shame will lead to one bad decision after another and take you down the wrong road quickly. This, in turn, provides the enemy a prime opportunity to convince you of the lie that you're too bad or too far gone for God to love you, much less use you in any significant way.

Our all-powerful God redeems the lost and the hurting every day. If you're struggling with guilt, He can help. The first step is to confess to God what you've done to cause the guilt and receive the forgiveness He offers. Romans 3:23, says, "All have sinned and fall short of the glory of God." However, verse 24 goes on to say, "They receive God's approval freely by an act of his kindness through the price Christ Jesus paid to set us free from sin."[6]

On the cross, Jesus took our sin upon Himself and became a living sacrifice for the sin that causes and feeds our guilt—a guilt that can and will kill us. Through His death, we are righteous and no longer enslaved to our sin. We give Christ our sin and, in return He gives us a whole and eternal life. Because of that exchange, God declares us "not guilty." It doesn't matter what you've done; it only matters what Jesus has done for you. It doesn't matter how bad you think you are; it only matters how good Jesus is. Whenever you hold on to your guilt, you're actually telling God that His death wasn't enough—that you need also to pay for your sin personally in addition to what He accomplished on the cross. This is another lie of the enemy.

Colossians 2:13–14 says, "He has forgiven you all your sins: Christ has utterly wiped out the damning evidence of broken laws and commandments which always hung over our heads, and has completely annulled it by nailing it over his own head on the cross."[7] The word *annulled* means that an action once made is reversed as though it never happened. That's what Jesus' death and resurrection has done for humankind—annulled our sin. When you confess your sin, and ask Him to forgive you, He forgives you completely.

Yes, He wants us to have a healthy sorrow over any of the sins we have committed, but this godly sorrow should lead to conviction and desire to change our behavior rather than fear, guilt, and condemnation. Because Jesus nailed your sin to the cross, you can quit nailing yourself over your sin. It's been canceled, reversed, annulled—

however you choose to look at it—so you can live free from the guilt that binds and weighs you down. My move to Utah was frustrating when I realized I was what needed to change. It's also the moment I began to understand that Christ was the *only* One who could remove my guilt. This revelation changed everything in my life moving forward, including my need to run away from myself.

Second: Allow God to Replace Your Grudge.

In the previous section, I talked about the guilt and pain we inflict on ourselves, but we are not always the source of our pain; sometimes, it is caused by other people. Whether others hurt us intentionally or not, it's easy and most natural to internalize anger and form a grudge. I think we all know the definition of the noun form of the word *grudge*: a persistent feeling of ill will or resentment toward someone. But the definition of the verb form is, to be resentfully unwilling to give, grant, or allow. A grudge is linked to anyone in your life that you haven't freely or fully forgiven.

A grudge causes bitterness that can lead to a gamut of other negative emotions. Martin Luther King Jr. said that bitterness is blindness, which results in clouded judgment.[8] A grudge will often lead to resentment and offense on our part. But God tells us to extend to others what has been extended by Jesus to us . . . His forgiveness.

If you are holding a grudge right now, I certainly don't want to minimize any injustice someone has placed on you, and the thought of forgiveness may seem completely inappropriate based on how you feel toward the other party. There are some situations that I would refer to as abuse that leave deep wounds that require ongoing counseling. Although the ultimate goal is twofold—first healing, then forgiveness—sometimes simply releasing a grudge without counseling can be more hurtful than helpful. If you have been in a relationship that was abusive, exploitative, or anything else of that magnitude, I recommend counseling to guide you in your healing.

If you are currently in this type of destructive relationship, especially a physically abusive one, exiting the relationship for your own safety is the first step toward healing. No one deserves to be hurt at the hands of a "loved one." God desires to help us heal, and a big part of our healing begins when we follow Him to a place of physical safety. A destructive relationship with a feeling of entrapment does not echo the heart of God for any His children. He desperately loves you no matter what has happened and desires total healing for you. Sometimes the hardest thing for someone to acknowledge is that He desires their safety more than He desires the relationship that is causing physical harm.

I am convinced that healing and forgiveness happen in tandem, but each individual must assess their own situation or enlist the help of a licensed counselor to see which one needs to happen first. This is where good counselors can really help to steer us in the right direction toward God's ultimate goal of healing. At the point of healing, consider Jesus' challenge of forgiveness, even as He forgave those who so brutally abused Him on the cross. In fact, forgiveness at the end of a season of counseling, or even as a goal of counseling, could be the greatest medicine to heal old and deep wounds. But remember, if we make decisions with the mind of Christ, forgiveness is actually not a feeling. It is a choice, and a logical one at that.

Unforgiveness, or holding a grudge, doesn't hurt the other person; it only hurts you. We may think *I'll show you* by not forgiving them, but with unforgiveness, we are actually giving them power to continue their offense. It's the equivalent of throwing gasoline on a bonfire within our soul. Instead of removing our pain, we inflict more pain upon ourselves. Nelson Mandela once said, "Resentment is like drinking poison and then hoping it will kill your enemies."[9] Unforgiveness allows the other person to actually control your life.

Think about it in a simple scenario. You are at a party, and the person you have not forgiven walks in the door. You decide to walk out the back door because you don't want to be in the same room with him, much less enjoy yourself at the same party. Wherever he goes, you avoid him, demonstrating that he actually has control over you. He gets to stay and join in the fun with your friends, while you feel compelled to leave. Who is *really* losing in this scenario?

In John 8:36, Jesus says, "If the Son sets you free, you will be free indeed." When Jesus says "you will be free indeed," He means freedom in every area of your life—including freedom from your grudges.

In Luke 4:18, Jesus is quoting from Isaiah, talking about His purpose (with my emphasis):

> The Spirit of the Lord is on me,
> because he has anointed me
> to proclaim good news to the poor.
> He has sent me to proclaim *freedom for the prisoners*
> and recovery of sight for the blind,
> *to set the oppressed free.*

Jesus clearly preached good news to the prisoners, but that doesn't necessarily mean He handed out "Get out of jail free" cards. Jesus is certainly able to deliver us from physical prisons, including bad relationships, but He is also able to deliver us from internal spiritual and emotional issues, such as unforgiveness.

Romans 12:19 says, "Do not take revenge, my dear friends, but leave room for God's wrath, for it is written: 'It is mine to avenge; I will repay,' says the Lord." When it comes down to it, will you trust and believe what the Lord Himself says? When we simply take Him at His word, believing He'll do exactly what He says He'll do, we can truly relinquish our grudges into His care and receive the healing and freedom He wants to provide. Forgive others, let God deal with your offenders, and believe He will repay those according to their transgressions.

If you are not quite able to forgive yet, I encourage you to pray the prayer, "God, make me willing to forgive." He will empower you to do what He is calling you to do, every single time.

Third: Allow God to Relieve Your Grief.

Loss happens to everyone. Whether your grief is from the death of a loved one, the ending of a friendship, or the obliteration of a dream, this deep sorrow is an unavoidable part of our lives here on earth. When grief shows up in our lives, it's extremely important to allow our hearts and souls the proper time to grieve. Ecclesiastes 3:1, 4 says, "For everything there is a season . . . A time to cry and a time to laugh. A time to grieve and a time to dance."[10]

Grieving looks different to different people. As a pastor who is often faced with helping others during their grieving process, I always encourage people to be as raw and authentic as possible. It's not a time to censor your thoughts or words: God in His mercy understands. "The LORD is close to the brokenhearted and saves those who are crushed in spirit" (Psalm 34:18).

There are many effective ways to work through grief. It could be through journaling, like King David models in the Psalms. Taking a trip to withdraw from your normal responsibilities and allowing your heart to be open before God could be just what you need. Or you may just need to take long runs, play a sport, or engage in some other physical activity where you're able to externally express and release what has built up internally. Oftentimes the best way to process your grief is by talking with a counselor, pastor, or close friend who gives you the space to express your thoughts or simply sits with you in silence. Job's friends model this in Job 2:13: "They sat on the ground with him for seven days and seven nights. No one said a word to him, because they saw how great his suffering was." A friend who does this with you is nothing less than a gift from God.

At the time of my burnout, I was not dealing with significant grief in my life. I had things in my life to grieve over, but I was not stopping long enough to process who and what had been lost along the way. All this changed when I resigned from Metro Church. I deeply loved that church, the amazing people, and the wonderful staff. It took ten years of my life, almost every waking hour, to nurture and lead it from nothing to almost six thousand members. When I had time to finally reflect, I realized that I had sadly spent more time raising the church than I had raising all four of my children combined. I believe my grief was almost on par with David's in the loss of his child. I quickly realized that the grief I felt was like losing a fifth child.

To bring the points of guilt, grudge, and grief together, I like to look at the Celtic cross, an ancient representation of forgiveness that originated in Ireland. In fact, this particular symbol was originally known as the forgiveness cross because of the way it is designed, depicting the three different areas where forgiveness needs to be extended.

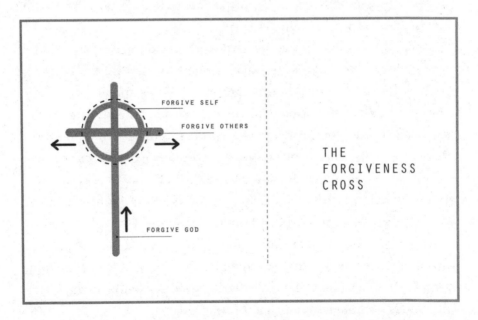

The vertical piece of the cross is forgiveness extended between us and God. The whole of our faith is based on the forgiveness that is extended from God down to us, representing the path to heaven made accessible to us through Christ's sacrifice on the cross. Through our confession of sin, we can be forgiven by the Father because of Christ's finished work on the cross. (See 1 John 1:9.) As a secondary path of forgiveness on this same vertical piece of the cross, our forgiveness is interpreted as an act of devotion and extended back to God, signified by the arrow pointing up. When we first become a follower of Christ, there is often an initial zeal and excitement about God. In this joyous and forgiven season, we would never think of getting angry at God. However, after a harder season, we may find the need to extend our forgiveness back to God for some hardship that has happened to us along the way. This forgiveness is not merited by Him, nor are our hardships His doing, but sometimes, without knowing what else to do with our pain, we have a tendency to place blame on Him. Forgiving God sounds like a huge subject to interject in this simple illustration, but sometimes it is the biggest area that forgiveness needs to be extended. If we have a grudge against God, this can create an unnecessary wedge between us and Him that can cause doubt and mistrust instead of the hope and faith He desires for us to have in Him and His plans for our lives. Is there something that has happened in your life that you need to forgive God for?

The horizontal part of the Celtic cross represents the forgiveness we now extend to others in our lives. Since we freely received forgiveness from God, we freely extend forgiveness to those around us. (See Ephesians 4:32.)

The circle intersecting the horizontal and vertical lines represents Jesus' head—His mind—while hanging on the cross. I don't think man is capable of knowing or understanding what went on in Jesus' head while He was dying, but we do know that His death was necessary for removing our guilt. When we are able to receive God's forgiveness, our guilt is removed and, in turn, we can forgive others and ourselves. It is a circle of events that brings healing, restoration, and a Whole Life rhythm to our emotions.

There are no easy answers for life's most difficult scenarios, but God is not only grieved over the pain and loss that we experience; He's also grieved when we blame Him and turn away from the comfort and hope He wants to provide. How the sovereignty of God and the consequences of man's free will work together is one of the most complex mysteries of the universe. However, I am confident of His promise that He will work all things, even the hard and painful things, together for our good. As Tim Keller explains in his book *Prayer*, "God will either give us what we ask or give us what we would have asked if we knew everything He knows."[11]

STEPS TO HEALING YOUR SOUL

David is considered a true hero of the faith, a man after God's heart. (See Acts 13:22.) But in 2 Samuel 12, in what is probably one of the most horrific, unfortunate stories in the entire Old Testament, David commits adultery and murders someone to cover up his sin. Then the prophet Nathan pays him a visit to tell him that his son will die because of his sin. David was dealing with grief in every area of his life. Not only was he feeling guilty about his sin, he probably had a bit of a grudge—maybe against Nathan, maybe against God.

Second Samuel 12:20–23 tells us that once his son had died, David got up from the ground, cleaned himself up, spent some time in worship, and went home for dinner. His son was already dead. While his son was still living, he fasted and wept. He did everything spiritually and physically that he could do. But, David said, "now that he is dead, why should I go on fasting? Can I bring him back again?" (verse 23). From this passage we see David moved on after he acknowledged his son was gone. During his time of fasting, weeping, and prayer, David was probably processing his own shame and how his sin could so greatly affect someone he loved so dearly as he moved toward accepting the reality of what had happened. In the midst of all his mess, David set a pattern that I believe we can follow as a true prescription for how to allow God into these areas. As I followed this pattern when processing my own grief of losing Metro

Church, I, too, found that God used it in a powerful way to fully re-lieve my grief. This pattern will not only help you to receive God's healing for your grief; it will also bring the same healing for your guilt and grudge.

STEP ONE: Accept What Can't be Changed

David realized the first step to healing is accepting what can't be changed. In caring for our souls and following God's prescription for whole emotions, there are some things that are beyond our control. You can either continue to feel guilty, have a grudge about it, or even grieve about it, but at the end of the day, if you want to experience emotional wholeness, you are going to have to accept what cannot be changed.

STEP TWO: Lay It Down and Begin to Shift into a Season of Prayer

Like David, you can decide to lay down the thing you cannot change. You have a choice in life. You can either exaggerate the issues in your mind and let your thoughts run wild, or you can dedicate them to the Lord. All of us are gifted at dreaming up worst-case scenarios—thoughts about what could or might happen in a situation, or may never happen. My own experience has been that the worst-case scenarios I dream up never materialize and consistently waste my time and mental energy!

Have you noticed that you have a higher propensity to make emotional decisions in certain circumstances? There is an acrostic I learned in grad school that can help us to make decisions that are not purely based in emotion called HALT: Hungry, Angry, Lonely, Tired. Whenever you find yourself in any of these circumstances, I strongly encourage you *not* to make a decision.

Hungry. When I am hungry, not only am I more likely to buy a package of Oreos when I go to the grocery store, but I am more likely to say something out of frustration that I don't really mean. One of my former staff members used to have a funny sign on her desk that said, "Forgive me for what I said when I was hungry." It's true! *Hangry* has become a part of our vocabulary for a reason.

Angry. In a marriage or in any other relationship, don't have an important discussion when you are angry. You may need to talk through something that just happened, but save the deeper processing for later. When you are angry, you will say and do things that you will later regret when the anger has subsided and your blood pressure has returned to normal.

Lonely. I also don't recommend making decisions when you are lonely. The enemy is always trying to make you feel like an island separate from everyone. As a member of the body of Christ, you are never meant to be isolated, nor are you ever meant to make decisions apart from your relationship with God. However, there are times where you may feel disconnected from God and your community. Re-engage in your relationship with Him and purposely seek out God-first friendships; don't make your decisions in a relational vacuum. As Proverbs 11:14 says, "Where no counsel is, the people fall: but in the multitude of counselors there is safety" (KJV).

Tired. We can only make one good decision when we are tired—to go to sleep.

As you dedicate an issue to God, symbolically laying it down at His altar, you are giving it back to Him. After David washed up, he changed his clothes and went into the house of the Lord to worship. He was communicating to God and the world that he had accepted his son was dead and that he had messed up royally. Accepting what he could not change, he decided to dedicate it, to lay it down. He worshipped because he knew that God was still good, despite his own failings.

David could have been paralyzed by guilt. It was his decision to sleep with Bathsheba, when she was another man's wife, that led to

Bathsheba's pregnancy. He could have also had a significant grudge toward God for allowing the baby to die shortly after birth. Instead, David took the high road and sincerely grieved over the loss of his child. He laid down his grief, his guilt, and his grudge, choosing instead to hand it all over to God in prayer.

After David laid his burden down before God, he shifted into a lifestyle of prayer, as evidenced by Psalm 51, which was written right after he committed adultery. He lays down his grief in verse 12 when he asks God to restore the joy of his salvation, and he lays down his guilt in verse 14 when he prays, "Deliver me from the guilt of bloodshed . . ." We also see that David does not seem to harbor hurt or bitterness toward God: "Open my lips, Lord; and my mouth will declare your praise" (verse 15).

I believe David made the one decision that is a telltale sign of spiritual maturity: going directly to God and allowing Him to take his pain instead of fleeing from Him. Worship is simply magnifying the Lord by letting Him know you know how big He is. Whenever you worship God, instead of running from Him, you run to God; instead of allowing your challenges to turn into great misery in life, laying them down before Him allows Him to turn your problems into a brand-new, fresh perspective of the road ahead.

Whenever your feelings are the thing leading the charge, it's often difficult to have a clear perspective. You can only see the road ahead when your soul is restored to the way God intended.

STEP THREE: *Focus on What's Left, Not What's Lost*

Once you lay down the thing you cannot change and begin to pray, the last step is to focus on what is left, not what is lost. As a pastor, I often meet with people who are looking at life in the rearview mirror. You can't move forward down the road if you are constantly looking backward at what you lost. At some point in time you are going to have to look forward and focus on what is left.

Second Samuel 12:24 says, "Then David comforted his wife Bathsheba, and he went to her and made love to her. She gave birth to a son, and they named him Solomon." Solomon was the guy who was the heir to the throne. He is the one who ended up building the temple that David wasn't allowed to build. Solomon picked up and moved forward with his father's legacy. What this tells us is that God is not done with you, no matter what has happened, if you accept what can't be changed.

David chose not to remain stuck in guilt for his decision to sleep with Bathsheba. He chose not to become overcome with grief over the loss of his child. And he chose not to develop a grudge against God for allowing his child to die. He decided to focus on what was left—his new wife and, eventually, his new child—not on what was lost. Whenever you focus on what is left, you are going to find there is a whole lot more left than you ever dreamed. We can move forward confidently, knowing God has really good things ahead for us. I believe God is telling us, just as God instructed Joshua (Joshua 1:9): "Be strong and courageous. Do not be afraid; do not be discouraged, for the Lord your God will be with you wherever you go."

POSITION YOURSELF ON SOLID GROUND

One of the best ways to keep your soul right sided and to position yourself on solid ground is to surround yourself with close Christian friendships. One of my favorite life messages is teaching people the importance of having three close Christian friends. I do not believe you can experience the whole life God intended for you without them.

There was a study done recently by the American Church Research Project that indicated the greatest statistical predictor of spiritual growth in a believer's life is having a few close, authentic friendships with those who are also trying to grow in their relationship with God.[12]

Your spirit tank is not the only tank that will benefit from having close, God-first friendships. They are also vital to your soul care. I watched a fascinating segment on the *Today* show recently about the positive benefits of having close friends in your life. They shared a study done at the University of Virginia where they placed people in an anxiety-producing situation and tested their stress levels when their best friend held their hand, when a stranger held their hand, and when they were alone. It is probably not surprising that they were most stressed when they were alone, but I found it interesting that holding a stranger's hand only slightly reduced their anxiety. What I found the most fascinating was that even in high anxiety-producing situations, they showed no visible signs of anxiety or stress when they were holding their best friend's hand.[13]

This study reinforces the truth that you were not meant to walk through this life alone. You were made to be in relationship. I believe God desires this for you, and He will help you find these individuals if you do not already have them in your life. We see this modeled in Jesus' life. Although he had a genuine friendship with all of his disciples, He invited Peter, James, and John to be His inner circle. We all need an inner circle of at least three.

Although I recommend processing with God first, it is very important to share your authentic, unedited feelings with those who are in your inner circle. Remember, it can take time to build these relationships. You want to surround yourself with people you feel safe with and who you can fully trust. You also want these friends to be in a close relationship with God, since they will be speaking into your life and helping your soul to stay healthy.

They should know the ungodly beliefs that you have wrestled with and the godly beliefs that they were replaced with so they can remind you whenever you forget. They should know your God-first priorities so they can help make sure you are staying in alignment with His will. These are friends you should be 100 percent real with so that they can speak truth into your life when you get off course.

I know these friendships have been invaluable in my life; although not perfect, they have helped me to unpack my emotions and examine what is going on in my soul. They ask me probing questions and provide a safe space for me to share. They help me uncover the guilt, grudges, or grief in my heart that I need to release to God. I can confidently say that even though these types of conversations didn't come naturally to me at first, they have become the greatest catalysts for emotional health in my life.

Over the past few years I have learned how to process my thoughts, my decisions, and my emotions in a healthy way so that intentional soul care is now a regular part of my life. If you have heavier issues to process or need specialized help, I advise finding a local licensed counselor or a Christian ministry that focuses on soul care. Reach out to a clergy member or leader at your church for recommendations.

God offers you the path to have whole and balanced emotions, and His blessing rests on you when your soul is in the correct order. If you have an inverted soul where your emotions are governing your will and mind, ask Him to restore you to His right order, where your soul is led by the mind of Christ, the will of God, and then the feelings that God desires for you.

REVIEW

In this chapter I discussed the danger of living with unprocessed emotions, and what I call an inverted soul. Your soul is inverted when you are led by your emotions—suppressed or out of control—instead of by your spirit and the will of God.

To restore an inverted soul, I spoke about dealing with any guilt in your life, allowing God to replace your grudges by forgiving anyone who offended or sinned against you, and allowing God to relieve your grief.

Through David's story we saw that he had to accept what he couldn't change, lay his burden down and shift into a season of prayer, let God give him a new perspective on his circumstances, and focus on what he had left. Doing these four things in your own life will ensure that you are allowing God to restore your soul. Although these steps may take time, remember: God's desire is total freedom and your end result in this process will be nothing short of it.

WHOLE LIFE CHALLENGE

To help you grow emotionally in your Whole Life journey, I encourage you to find three close Christian friends with whom you can share transparently. You may already have this type of relationship with your Whole Life partner or small group at your church. If you don't have these friendships yet, take proactive steps toward developing them. These individuals will not be perfect, but they should be people who are living an evident God-first life, will pray with you and for you, and have the ability to speak into your life. On your Whole Life journey, finding a rhythm, not perfection, is the key. With that said, set times when you can consistently meet with these close Christian friends and you will begin to find a rhythm in your soul as a critical part of your Whole Life journey.

I encourage you to meet with one of your friends each week and model transparency. Don't just share with them what happened during your week; also share how you felt during the week. Below are some sample questions for you to answer as you share with your friends. By sharing your answers with them and encouraging them to share their answers with you, you will begin to take your friendships deeper through the power of transparency.

1. What positive thing made you feel good this week? Was there anything that made you sad or disappointed?

2. What was your overall emotional state this week? What caused any highs or lows, and how did you walk through them?

3. Were you emotionally present with those closest to you this week? Did you share openly with them?

4. Did you have any emotional echoes this week, where you feel like you had a stronger emotional reaction than the situation warranted?

5. Did you experience guilt, grudges, or grief this week? Have you released these, or are you in the process of working through any of these?

After taking these steps, you are sure to make huge strides toward finding a Whole Life rhythm in your emotions, not to mention a fully restored soul.

part three

Body Health

FIRST THESSALONIANS 5:23 talks about our spirits, souls, *and* bodies. Our bodies house our spirits and souls and connect us to the world around us through our five senses. They influence how our spirits and souls feel, as a weak or ill body can affect the mind and emotions, and even drag us down spiritually.

In the introduction, I shared how I had neglected my bodily health for many years. I was overworked, overweight, and burned-out. I had gone from a solid thirty-two-inch waist in college to a thirty-six over the course of fifteen years. In fact, the pants section of my closet looked like a department store, with an array of different sizes. While I'd been busy filling up my spirit tank, my body suffered. As I began to understand more about the interconnectedness of all three parts of our whole selves, I realized that taking proper care of our bodies is an act of stewardship before God.

We get the idea of stewardship from Paul's comment that we are not our own but were bought with a price. In 1 Corinthians 6:19–20, Paul says, "Do you not know that your bodies are temples of the Holy Spirit, who is in you, whom you have received from God? You are not your own; you were bought at a price. Therefore honor God with your bodies." *Temple* is another word for sanctuary, or the dwelling place of God.

When Jesus rose from the grave, He returned to heaven, but then sent the Holy Spirit to live inside of you. When you confess and repent of your sin, receive the gift of forgiveness, and submit your life to Christ, the Holy Spirit takes up residence in your human spirit. That means the Spirit of God lives in our bodies—His temple—from the moment of salvation. We now belong to Him.

Because of His presence and ownership of our lives, we should honor God with our bodies. In fact, honoring God with your body is a form of worship to God. That means taking care of your "temple" so that the Spirit of God has a healthy and strong vessel to work in as you pursue His will for your life. You have big dreams, and He has equally big plans for your time on planet Earth. Since your body is the vessel that His Spirit will work through, it is important that you keep yours strong and healthy to fulfill His purposes. As with all the sections in this book, I am going to focus on three areas that will improve the overall health of your body while establishing some lifestyle attributes that will help you to increase your Whole Life rhythm. These three areas are nutrition, fitness, and rest.

While growing up, I was athletically inclined and played all sports. Body health was not a great concern, because no matter what I ate or drank, it seemed like I could function on anything as fuel. As I transitioned into adulthood, I found that my eating choices, lack of exercise, and lack of rest did not yield the same results. In fact, as I mentioned in the introduction, with the onset of Graves' disease, I was forced to pay attention to my health and recover from my dilapidated condition.

I'm not a medical doctor, but I feel like my personal journey toward a Whole Life rhythm as well as the tips I will share from nutritionists and fitness experts will add great benefit to anyone desiring to improve in these areas. Please note: If you have specific injuries, or health conditions or concerns, I encourage you to consult your doctor first.

My results have been nothing short of extraordinary, and today I am living a healthy lifestyle. At the time of writing this book, I have been given a clean bill of health, no longer having PTSD symptoms, and my Graves' disease is now well under control.

As I reflected over my personal journey to a whole life, I recognized three distinct phases that I experienced as I sought to integrate each area into my Whole Life rhythm:

1. **High-intensity phase:** This is the go-for-broke phase where serious change is necessary to fix something that is broken or nonexistent—something that you have not been stewarding well. The goal is to reset your daily habits and prepare your body for change. This phase is usually necessary when you are facing chronic illness, mental and physical exhaustion, or weight issues. This phase can last anywhere from a few weeks to a year or longer, depending on your base level of body health and your personal goals.

2. **Goal realization phase:** In this phase you begin to achieve your initial goals. You will have lost weight (if needed), improved your health and stamina, and begun to include regular seasons of rest into your life. As the areas you have been working on begin to integrate themselves more naturally into your life, the momentum and intensity levels off a bit. While the high-intensity phase focused on jump-starting habits that were not already a part of your life, the focus of this stage is to incorporate these new activities into a sustainable lifestyle. This phase usually lasts for twelve to twenty-four months.

3. **Whole Life rhythm phase:** In this phase, all three interconnected tanks are filling evenly together. Nutrition, fitness, and rest have become central to your physical life, and your body health no longer weighs down your spirit and soul. Your new lifestyle that incorporates body health is now in a rhythm that has become fully sustained. You will hopefully maintain this phase for your whole life.

This section may be the most challenging part of your Whole Life journey; it was for me. However, it is also the most practical in its application. Know that as you make changes in your lifestyle, desiring to honor God and steward the body He has given you, He will guide you, strengthen you, and bring you the support you need to succeed! Remember the goal for each person will be different, as each of our bodies is different. But keep in mind that the goal of this book is not to achieve perfection, with all three tanks completely full, but simply to help bring all these areas of a person into alignment in order to gain a Whole Life rhythm in your spirit, soul, and body. The area of body health is critical to this rhythm. As Ralph Waldo Emerson famously said, "The first wealth is health."

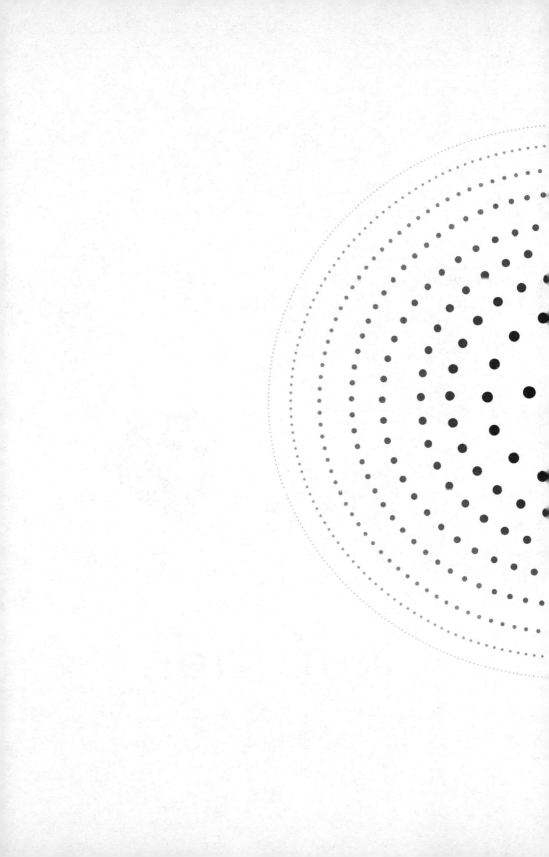

the
whole
life

Nutrition

eight

Nutrition—You Are What You Eat

Let food be thy medicine and medicine be thy food.
—Hippocrates

Whether you eat or drink or whatever you do, do it all for the glory of God.
—The Apostle Paul, 1 Corinthians 10:31

Nutrition has not been a priority for most of my life. My mom didn't care for cooking, so my siblings and I strongly identify with the fast-food generation. Our home phone had Domino's Pizza on speed dial, we made a "run for the border" to the Taco Bell drive-through quite frequently, and the "golden arches" hovered over many of our precious dining room table moments. Heck, I even had my birthday party at a McDonald's once.

In elementary school I learned about the major food groups and the recommended daily allotments in the food pyramid. I was obviously no nutritionist, but even I could see the stark difference between my diet and the USDA's recommendations.

Up until about five years ago, the two main "food groups" I chose to eat were pizza and burgers. I could easily devour a medium pepperoni pizza by myself for lunch, and the employees knew me by name at my favorite burger joint. As you can imagine, I began to tip the scales and soon weighed upward of 235 pounds! This may or may not sound like much to you, but it was quite a bit for my six-foot frame and was 70 pounds more than what I weighed during college.

One day my wife, who has stayed in incredible shape our entire marriage, made a comment about how much my size had changed in the years she has known me. She was trying to compliment me by expressing that she liked me a little bigger, but all I heard was that she thought I was fat! The timing of this realization coincided with my 1 Thessalonians 5:23 epiphany, and I started to understand how important stewarding bodily health really is in order to successfully live a whole life.

If we compare our bodies to cars, food is the fuel we put into our body tanks to help them run efficiently so we can get from point A to point B in life. If you put substandard, cheap gas in your tank all the time or never change the oil, you shouldn't be surprised if your car runs sluggishly or makes frequent trips to the repair shop. The clichés like "Garbage in, garbage out" and "You are what you eat" exist because there is truth in them. What we choose to eat has a huge impact on our overall health.

You may have ranked yourself low in the area of nutrition on your Whole Life Wheel. You may even share my former food preferences or struggle with weight that is significantly higher than what you reported on your driver's license. Or maybe weight is not the issue for you but your body is sick and tired, possibly from not choosing the right foods.

Change is possible, but you may need to take some serious steps to turn your situation around, like consulting with a nutritionist, doctor, or weight-loss specialist. Once you experience the benefits of eating right, you'll notice how much better you feel. If you scored high in this key area of the Whole Life Wheel, let this chapter be the confirmation for your healthy lifestyle choices and a challenge to you to find new information to take your body health to the next level. With a strong commitment to a Whole Life rhythm for your body, you can lose weight, increase your energy level, and raise the nutrition number on your Whole Life Wheel.

HIGH-INTENSITY PHASE

The high-intensity phase of nutrition is just that—a body reboot—and involves making some significant changes in order to see improvement in overall health. I know from personal experience that this can be really difficult. I found I had neglected the area of nutrition and exercise for such a long time, dramatic change in my nutrition was needed in different seasons to help reboot my body. I'd try one nutritional strategy but had difficulty maintaining it long term. Maybe you've struggled with the same problem. What ultimately worked for me turned out to be a unique combination of what I had tried.

My first experience with a high-intensity phase of nutrition happened in 2005. Years prior, in 1993, I was diagnosed with a digestive tract ailment called ulcerative colitis, a debilitating disease similar to Crohn's disease. My symptoms included abdominal pain, regular nausea, on and off internal bleeding, and unpredictable diarrhea. I had quarterly checkups, including an annual colonoscopy, to examine my digestive tract, but with no known cure, I had accepted the disease as a permanent part of my life. Once I became a Christian, I even tried to overspiritualize my chronic pain by calling it "a thorn in my flesh."

So, in January of 2005, while working as an associate pastor at a church in Jacksonville, Florida, Taryn and I participated in the start of their New Year fast. Our pastor invited our congregation to partner with God during that time and ask Him to do something miraculous in our lives. Taryn, having just witnessed a particularly bad episode of my colitis, suggested we should pray and fast for complete healing in my body. Because of my love for my wife, I agreed, but I was secretly resigned to the fate of living with this disease for the rest of my life.

Taryn found a book called *The Maker's Diet* by Jordan Rubin, which outlined an eating plan based on the dietary requirements found in the Old Testament book of Leviticus. Jordan's personal account of his battle and triumph over Crohn's disease resonated with me. I didn't expect any change in my condition, but I went along with Taryn's excitement, admiring her total faith that God would provide a breakthrough. I was relieved when we completed the intense twenty-one-day dietary elimination plan. Afterward, I went back to life as usual, not realizing what God had done in my body during those three weeks.

The following month I went in for my routine quarterly checkup with my gastroenterologist. After running the usual tests, he came back into the examination room with a look of complete bewilderment in his eyes.

"David," he said, "I can't explain this, but it's like you have a brand-new colon." He went on to explain that there was no trace of the disease in my body and the ulcers and the scars on my colon had completely vanished. I could not believe it! The news seemed too good to be true, but I knew this was an incredible, unexpected gift from God. I raced home to tell my wife and we celebrated the miracle that was ushered in by a drastic change in my diet.

I am blessed to have not had any further digestive complications since the shift in my diet, and the change brought about by this fast planted the seed of knowledge that there *is* a correlation that exists between what food I put in my body and how my body functions. While I can't promise you healing as dramatic as I've experienced, I can promise that if you steward your body properly, there is no limit to what God can or will do.

My next experience with a high-intensity phase of nutrition happened nine years later, in 2014, when we discovered my second son, Josiah, was gluten intolerant. I was in a season of having reverted back to poor eating habits and my scale was now registering the most pounds I had ever weighed. We decided this needed to be a family affair, as we believed it was unfair to remove all gluten from Josiah's diet and allow him to watch his siblings eat all sorts of glutenous treats. There was a significant learning curve for the whole family and a lot of time spent studying the gluten-free shelves at our grocery store, but after the initial shock of the first month I began to notice the benefits.

For as long as I can remember, I averaged two to three headaches a week. I simply assumed this was hereditary and kept a stash of Advil Liqui-Gels at my office, in my car, and at home, because the onset was always unpredictable for my headaches. About seven days into our new gluten-free diet, I realized I had not taken any Advil for the entire week. As my weeks progressed with no headaches, I realized this gluten-free diet was the reason.

Another benefit of going gluten-free was weight loss, specifically in my belly. I also found more sustained energy throughout the day and stopped falling into a "food coma" after meals. I followed the gluten-free diet for about a year but stopped once my crazy work and travel schedule made following it too challenging for me. To this day my wife has continued to make most of our family dinners gluten-free.

Finally, in January 2017, with the discovery of my Graves' disease, my doctor asked me to revisit my diet and make several nutritional modifications. I took what I had learned and benefited from in *The Maker's Diet* and our family's gluten-free diet, incorporating them into my current eating habits. I'm currently on a low-calorie/high-protein diet. I haven't completely eliminated gluten, but it is restricted, and I limit processed foods while giving preference to foods that are in their most natural state.

Perhaps the craziest part of my new diet is the complete elimination of coffee. I made the decision to quit and went cold turkey. I experienced headaches for the next few days but replaced my constant cups of coffee with bottles of water. As the caffeine worked its way out of my system, I was surprised and pleased by how good my body felt. I have had no desire for coffee after kicking the habit. While I don't believe coffee is necessarily bad, it needed to be cut from my diet because of my high heart rate and stress levels. At the time I gave it up, I was averaging three Venti Starbucks double shots a day.

Through the combined efforts of my new eating plan and exercise routines, I dropped 20 pounds in the first three months. Over the course of nine months, my weight dropped below 200 pounds for the first time in twenty years. I ended up landing at 185 pounds, which is right in the middle of the weight range for my height and frame.

It is hard to believe that I have lost a total of 50 pounds through this process and I am already well on my way to my ultimate goal of losing 70 pounds total. I am also pleased to share that due to this process my love handles now have a lot less grip, and my waist size shrank from 36 inches back down to the 32 inches I had back in high school. For the first time in decades, I finally feel confident and vibrant in my body. Because I started eating in a way that supported my bodily health, I began to experience true physical vitality. Not only was I healthier, but the food tastes delicious as well. And for the first time in my married life, when my wife and I go on a date to a restaurant, we order the same things. I have finally found a Whole Life rhythm for nutrition that works for me and my body.

In the following sections, I want to share with you what I've learned about the goal realization phase and help you find your Whole Life Rhythm as well.

GOAL REALIZATION PHASE

The high-intensity phase is usually not sustainable over the long term. For example, the extreme gluten-free diet we followed when Josiah was first identified as having a gluten intolerance was very expensive for our family to maintain. I also found that I had attained the goals I wanted to reach in that first intense phase and then quickly reached a plateau in my weight loss. I was much healthier than I had ever been, but I still desired to lose additional weight to be within the range for my height and size. This moved me into what I refer to as the goal realization phase of nutrition.

For the goal realization phase, you will begin to focus on stewarding your nutritional choices for the long haul and developing habits
that are sustainable for your lifestyle while still allowing freedom in
your choices. From my personal experience and the advice of nutritionists, I've pinpointed the three following areas that I encourage
you to focus on in the goal realization phase:

1. Eating whole, unprocessed foods

2. Getting proper hydration

3. Taking nutritional supplements

Let's look at each of these areas in more detail.

1. Eating Whole, Unprocessed Foods

Tony Horton, creator of the popular P90X video workout program, is
a great example of someone whose health was drastically improved
by following a sustainable diet. I consider myself to be someone who
has benefited from diet and exercise, but by no means am I a certified expert in these areas, so I interviewed Tony for this book. In the
interview, I learned that Tony stays lean and healthy by *not* starving
himself: He actually eats five meals a day, which keeps his body fueled
for his many workouts. His secret to eating all day and not getting
fat is more about *what* you eat; every morsel matters.[1] Tony's number
one nutrition tip is to eat more whole, unprocessed foods and to steer
clear of sugar.

Here are his examples of good sources of proteins, carbs, and
healthy fats:

Good Sources of Protein: Your body uses protein to build
and repair tissues. You also use proteins to make enzymes,
hormones, and other body chemicals. Protein is an im-

portant building block of bones, muscles, cartilage, skin, and blood.[2] Some good sources of protein include eggs and egg whites, protein bars, turkey breasts, fish, and chicken breasts. Lean meats are also a good source as long as you don't get the packaged, precooked meat, as it has too many preservatives.

Good Sources of Carbs: Foods high in carbohydrates are an important part of a healthy diet. Carbohydrates provide the body with glucose, which is converted to energy used to support body functions and physical activity.[3] Good sources of carbohydrates include whole grain/whole wheat breads (gluten-free as needed), fruits (apples, bananas, strawberries, etc.), and hummus.

Good Sources of Healthy Fats: Healthy fats are essential to give your body energy and to support cell growth. They also help protect your organs and keep your body warm. Fats also help your body absorb some critical nutrients and produce important hormones.[4] Some good sources of healthy fats are almonds, walnuts, low-fat cheese, olive oil, coconut oil, and avocados.

While the focus of the high-intensity phase limits your diet options to address specific health issues, there is greater freedom and flexibility in this phase. Tony's list of proteins, carbs, and healthy fats gives you some options to start with. From this list, you can see that you don't need to starve to be healthy. Eat what will keep you running in a sustainable and healthy way, watch your portion sizes, and learn to stop eating when your body tells you it is full.

2. Getting Proper Hydration

The average adult body is composed of approximately 50 to 60 percent water. Drinking sufficient water every day is an important component of our body health. Most nutritional experts agree that we should drink at least half of our body weight in ounces every day. My current weight is 185 pounds, which means I should drink almost 100 ounces of water a day. Honestly, this is still sometimes an aspirational goal, but I have significantly increased my daily water intake. I keep bottled water in the fridge at my office, and usually a case of bottled water in the trunk of my car with at least three bottles in my passenger seat as a reminder while I drive each day. I challenge myself to drink several bottles throughout the day. Simply shifting whatever you currently drink to water is a significant and productive step toward your Whole Life rhythm when it comes to nutrition.

Hydration is crucial for proper cellular functioning at every level, which affects your body weight and your health. A study Tony Horton conducted on the importance of drinking water reported that 75 percent of Americans are chronically dehydrated. In 37 percent of Americans, the thirst mechanism is so weak that it is mistaken for hunger. That means a lot of us have been eating when we should have been drinking a tall glass of H_2O. [5]

Mild dehydration slows down your metabolism as much as 3 percent. When you drink cold water, your metabolic rate is increased as much as 30 percent, which makes it one of the easiest but often overlooked means for weight loss.[6] So if you find yourself hungry in the middle of the night, or before your next meal, instead of making a trip to the fridge to fill up on leftovers or a snack, try drinking a glass of cold water. Eight ounces of water has been shown to shut down hunger pangs for almost 100 percent of participants, according to a study performed at the University of Washington.[7]

When you don't drink a sufficient amount of water, it can also affect everything from your mental agility to your energy level. Have you ever felt fatigue in your body in the middle of the day, finding it difficult to focus on your computer screen or the pile of papers from your boss? Instead of that second cup of coffee, try a bottle of water.

Once you are properly hydrated, you may start to see some positive changes in your physical health. If you're experiencing back and joint pain, eight to ten glasses of water a day have been shown to significantly ease those pains in up to 80 percent of sufferers. And five glasses of water daily decreases the risk of colon cancer by 45 percent, breast cancer by 79 percent, and bladder cancer by 50 percent.[8]

Proper hydration, combined with a change in your diet, can have a dramatic effect on your physical health, stamina, and even your mental agility—all important to living a whole life.

3. Taking Nutritional Supplements

Many people I know use supplements and vitamins to enhance their nutrition. I often wondered why they were necessary if you eat a diet full of healthy, balanced foods. The answer is that we do not live in a perfect world and are often introduced to outside toxins, like the pesticides sprayed on crops and the preservatives put into our foods. Even if you try to eat right, you cannot always be 100 percent sure of what is in the food you are eating.

Registered dietitian Heather Fitzgerald, who is based in Los Angeles, recommends four must-have supplements to add to any diet, with the approval of your doctor or nutritionist:

1. Omega-3 Fatty Acids
Our bodies are pretty good at converting dietary fat into whatever other kind of fat it needs, but there are a couple kinds of

fat that the body can't make itself. These are called "essential fatty acids."[9]

Omega-3s, primary forms of essential fatty acids, can be found in salmon, beef, and even walnuts. Since they are harder to come by in our natural diet, a supplement is recommended. Omega-3s help lower the risk of heart attacks, curb joint pain, and can even help stabilize our moods. Whether you get omega-3s through your diet or a supplement, they are a big benefit to your body health.[10] If you can't find omega-3s in a pill, try cod liver oil or another fish oil to get your essential fatty acids.

2. Multivitamin

While it is not recommended that you live like George Jetson and get all your nutrients from a pill, taking a daily multivitamin is a great safety net.[11] A multivitamin ensures you get a combination of several of the main nutrients that your body needs on a daily basis.

I recommend going to your local health food or vitamin store to pick out a multivitamin that works for you. You can also check out my brand of supplements, The Whole Life Supplements, in a link included in the appendix of this book. After searching for supplements made from whole foods and finding no adequate options on the market, a close friend and I developed our own. Our supplements are made from whole ingredients that are also organic, gluten free, and vegan. My kids now enjoy our children's version called Tiger Bites. Taryn uses our probiotic supplement as well as the Women's Once Daily Multivitamin. I, on the other hand, use our Men's Once Daily Multivitamin. The most important thing to remember, regardless of which multivitamin you select, is that you take it consistently, integrating it into your Whole Life rhythm.

3. Vitamin D

Vitamin D is a fat-soluble vitamin that helps absorb calcium, which is crucial for maintaining bone density. This is especially important for women, who are more prone to osteoporosis as they age. Vitamin D has also been shown to help cells mature.[12]

My preferred method of vitamin D intake is the sun, but if you don't live in a temperate climate or have an office job, this can often be challenging, especially in the winter. When the weather is nice, I try to step out from the artificial, fluorescent lights in my office and walk outside for ten to fifteen minutes to soak up some vitamin D. But, depending on the weather and where you live, you can't always depend on the sun, so check out the vitamin D supplements available at your local health food store.

4. Probiotics

The human intestines contain millions of bacteria. Probiotics are the "good" bacteria that help digest certain foods, boost immunity, and help ward off cancer, allergies, and other autoimmune diseases.[13] Probiotics are naturally found in your body and in certain foods and supplements.

If you prefer not to take probiotics in supplement form, there is probiotic yogurt (Taryn likes this), fermented cheeses (Swiss, Gouda, Parmesan, Cheddar), some cottage cheeses, sauerkraut, and kombucha. Probiotics are especially important to take when you purge *good* bacteria from your system, like after taking antibiotics.[14]

If you are able to take only one of the supplements listed above due to expense or inconvenience, I recommend starting with the multivitamin. My favorite way to receive extra supplements is through a protein shake. I drink a protein shake that functions like a multivitamin for breakfast or lunch—and it tastes really good, too! If you want more information about which supplements are best for you, I recommend scheduling a visit to your local physician, a dietitian, or a nutritionist who can help you personalize your supplement intake and naturally integrate it into your Whole Life rhythm. When I found the right formulas for myself, I was surprised to find out how I was getting little to no vitamin D into my system, which is literally free if you schedule a little time in the sun just a few times a week.

The main purpose of the goal realization phase is to help you develop practices that will become a natural part of your lifestyle. Krista Stryker, a certified nutritionist and personal trainer, who I also had the privilege of interviewing for this book, recommends that you enact nutritional changes slowly. Don't try to go from eating fast food three times a day to cooking steamed broccoli and chicken at home for every meal. Small changes over time will make the biggest difference and allow you to stay healthy and fit for life, as opposed to just following a short-term diet. Try to cook at home as much as possible. Making your own food gives you more control over the food you eat and helps you monitor what you put into your body. I have benefited greatly by having a wife who is not only healthy in her own right but also loves to cook very healthy (and tasty!) meals for me and our kids.

It is also important to change the way you think about healthy food. If you want to be successful for the long haul, you will need to learn to enjoy what you eat. The good news is that healthy eating can be delicious. The way that you prepare the food, and the spices and herbs you add, will make all the difference in your eating experience. There are hundreds of recipes online and in cookbooks. Many cities now have a variety of health-conscious restaurants that use organic, local produce and meats or offer gluten-free, vegetarian, and vegan menus so that you can enjoy eating out without having to worry. Next time you eat out, just ask to see either their healthy choices menu or their gluten-free menu. Most restaurants have one or both of these menus readily available. To help you out even further, I have added a list of restaurants along with their lowest-calorie meal selection as of the writing of this book in the appendix.

Krista recommends the 80/20 rule when it comes to nutrition: Eat healthy about 80 percent of the time, but allow yourself some treats and other indulgences the other 20 percent of the time. This way of eating is very doable for most people because it doesn't require you to be on a super-strict diet, which ultimately leads to binge eating and feelings of failure. It allows for enough wiggle room that every person needs to stay sane and healthy in the long term.

Krista also shared what she calls her Big Ten Nutrition Tips, which I have elaborated on based on my personal experience:

1. Aim for 40 percent of your calories to be from carbohydrates, 30 percent from fats, and 30 percent from protein.

This doesn't have to be exact, but it is a good guideline to maintain so that while you are eliminating unhealthy fats, you are also building muscle.

2. Eat as many whole foods as possible.

Whole foods are foods that are as close to their original natural state as possible, like a fresh peach as opposed to canned peaches in syrup. Whole foods can be found at most non–fast-food restaurants if you are dining out. As for eating at home, there are an abundance of resources online that can help you develop a meal plan that fits your palate.

3. Include protein in every single meal.

This will help feed your muscles and regulate your blood sugar, i.e., how hungry and cranky you are. Some great sources of protein include eggs, turkey breasts, fish, chicken breasts, lean meats, and protein bars.

4. Eat often.

Aim for five to seven meals a day. This doesn't work for all people, but for people who are active, eating smaller portions every three to four hours is ideal for staying lean and maintaining energy levels and should stave off any sugary energy drink consumption in the afternoon times.

5. Embrace fats.

No, I am not encouraging you to gobble down handfuls of french fries. Healthy fats—like those found in avocados, nuts, and fish— are where it's at. Just a few years ago, the word *fat* was a bad word, but now we know it's really carbs and refined sugar that can be a problem.

6. Limit refined carbohydrates and processed food in general.

Refined carbs—like white bread, white rice, regular pasta (as opposed to whole-grain), and many breakfast cereals—can drive overeating and increase the risk of obesity. Because they are low in fiber and digest quickly, eating refined carbs can also cause major swings in blood sugar levels.

7. Eat fresh fruits and vegetables.

Rinse and repeat. According to the *2015–2020, Dietary Guidelines for Americans*, published by the U.S. Department of Health and Human Services and U.S. Department of Agriculture, you should consume "a variety of vegetables from all of the subgroups—dark green, red and orange, legumes (beans and peas), starchy, and . . . fruits, especially whole fruits."[15] Just about every day, Taryn will put out a couple of peeled and cut apples on a plate in our kitchen, and within an hour they are all gone. This has been a great trick to get our children to eat healthful foods and it has worked on them for years now.

8. No starving yourself if you're trying to lose weight.

From my own experience, extended fasts, no matter how well intended, are usually followed by gaining back the weight that was just starved out of you. Although I do believe a fast could be a great part of your high-intensity phase to reboot your nutrition and clean out your system of toxins, this is obviously no way to live indefinitely.

9. Don't deny yourself the things you love.

Save them for special times and you'll enjoy them even more. Obviously, holidays are not good times to start lifestyle eating changes. I have found that this type of eating plan can be rewards-based so that you can eat healthily and then still enjoy the things you love in moderation without feeling guilty.

10. Savor each meal.

Food is wonderful and is meant to be enjoyed! Just like you have favorite foods now, you will have favorites again in your new healthy eating plan.

A healthy lifestyle should be something that is enjoyable and sustainable. There definitely are some things you will need to stop consuming daily—like certain fast foods and sugary treats—but as you feed your body with what it needs and experience the benefits of feeling good, some of that unhealthy food will lose its appeal. And on the days where you treat yourself, you will enjoy it even more.

As an example, I enjoy a piece of cake during special occasions like my kids' birthday parties, but I am careful to monitor my consumption of gluten and my overall food intake. I'm now able to clearly see the direct correlation between my nutrition and my body health.

Your goal here is lifestyle change, so treat each meal as a restart. Give yourself some grace when you eat something unhealthy instead of throwing up your hands and calling it quits for the week. If you have an unhealthy lunch, simply have a healthier dinner. It's all about finding *your* rhythm. Once you start to eat more healthily, you'll realize how much better you feel. Your body will actually start to *crave* healthier foods. Remember, a sustainable rhythm, not perfection, is the goal that God has for us.

As you develop and steward a lifestyle of good nutrition in the goal realization phase, at some point you'll slip over into the Whole Life rhythm phase. This is when nutrition becomes a natural part of your lifestyle.

WHOLE LIFE RHYTHM PHASE

There are a variety of indicators that will signal when you have entered the Whole Life rhythm phase of nutrition. One indicator is that your weight will be within the recommended range for your height and frame, your energy level will be better than it's been in years, and you'll choose healthy foods without even thinking about it. Visits to fast-food chains will be a thing of the past, and you'll likely be taking a daily supplement or two.

At the writing of this book, I have been on my Whole Life plan for about two years. The great thing about this diet is that it is really not a diet at all but more of a nutritional lifestyle plan that leads to lasting change. I am not a huge fan of the idea of constant dieting, but I still use the plan that follows to this day. In fact, I actually eat more food than before and have gained muscle mass while losing the weight. As easy as this plan is, I would recommend having a quick visit with your doctor before embarking on it.

This nutritional lifestyle plan is all about the numbers, which you can alter by changing your food selection. In order to track your information, use a calorie tracking app or a simple journal like I do. Because I am very active—as mentioned, I am an avid tennis player—I need to focus on my calorie numbers and protein. In giving my body enough protein each day, it made me less hungry and also allowed my body to attack fat and leave my muscle alone to grow. Depending on your activity level, you can adjust your numbers accordingly.

———

Here are the three goals I suggest you pursue every week:

GOAL 1: **Eat less than your maintenance number of calories on a weekly basis.** Your maintenance number is the number of calories you need each day to sustain your current body composition. If you take in more than this number of calories, no matter what type of food, you will gain fat. If you consume less than this number of calories, you will lose fat. This is about 80 percent of the numbers in the equation and truly is the most important part of the equation. In fact, by getting this right first, your body will drop weight quickly even without completing goals two and three. However, from a wholeness standpoint, I really recommend goals two and three to keep your body in the best health possible.

Let's say your maintenance calories are 2,200 per day: 2,200 calories x 7 days = 15,400 calories. So if you eat 15,400 calories in a week, you will not gain or lose weight. One pound of body fat is equal to 3,500 calories. So to lose 2 pounds of fat per week (3,500 x 2), you need to reduce your calories for the week by 7,000 calories; 15,400 maintenance calories per week – 7,000 = 8,400 calories per week, or 1,200 calories per day. To lose 2 pounds of fat per week, you can eat 1,200 calories per day, or you can divide your weekly calories into five days and fast for two nonconsecutive days per week. (Please consult your doctor as needed when deciding what strategy will work well for you.)

I have listed some great foods in the appendix that work for this plan, and these were some of my favorites before I even started all this! It's really amazing that simply changing your mind about food selection will help your body to lose unwanted weight almost immediately.

GOAL 2: **Count your macros (protein, carbohydrates, and fat).** My goal, as a physically active person, is to lose body fat only and not any muscle. To preserve muscle in a caloric deficit, we need to eat close to 1 gram of protein per pound of lean body mass. Body mass is the estimated weight of your body without fat. Before I did this plan, I was roughly 185 pounds and an estimated 20 percent body fat. So multiply 185 × 80% = 148. I estimated up a little and I eat roughly 150g of protein every day. Most food is labeled in terms of grams of protein on the label so you should find it to be a somewhat easy process to estimate what your daily intake of protein is, especially if you are using protein bars and shakes to supplement your other meals each day.

To estimate your body fat, visit your physician or nutritionist. There are also body fat charts on the Internet that can help as a guideline. As a general rule when estimating your body fat, I recommend adding 10 to it. I didn't realize how much extra weight I was carrying around until I started getting lean. I thought I was 10 percent body fat when I was really more like 20 percent.

The following quiz will help you determine the number of calories you should be eating daily. Note that this quiz is based on the assumption that you are completing a high-intensity workout for forty-five minutes three days a week, and there is also the sedentary option on the chart if you are not doing a regular physical workout activity. Most people are surprised that it seems to recommend high caloric consumption, but it emphasizes that the type of calories you are eating and the frequency with which you are eating are crucial factors in being able to eat so many nutritious calories.

Answer and score the questions about your gender, weight, activity level, and weight goals, then compare your score with your recommended calorie plan, including protein, carbs, and fat.

the
whole
life

① WHAT'S YOUR GENDER?

FEMALE	ADD 1
MALE	ADD 2

② WHAT'S YOUR WEIGHT?

130 LBS. OR LESS	ADD 1
130 LBS. - 160 LBS.	ADD 2
161 LBS. - 180 LBS.	ADD 3
181 LBS. - 200 LBS.	ADD 4
201 LBS. - 220 LBS.	ADD 5
221 LBS. & UP	ADD 6

③ WHAT'S YOUR ACTIVITY LEVEL?

SLACKER (DESK JOB)	SUBTRACT 1
MODERATE (SERVER IN RESTAURANT)	ADD 0
HARDCORE (CONSTRUCTION WORKER)	ADD 1

④ MODIFIERS

WANT TO LOSE WEIGHT?	ADD 0
WANT TO MAINTAIN WEIGHT?	ADD 1
WANT TO ADD WEIGHT?	ADD 2

=TOTAL:

the
whole
life

YOUR SCORE

CALORIE PLAN

YOUR SCORE	CALORIE PLAN
2 OR LESS	PLAN A (1,500)
3	PLAN B (1,800)
4	PLAN C (2,100)
5	PLAN D (2,400)
6	PLAN E (2,700)
7 OR MORE	PLAN F (3,000)

	CALORIES	PROTEIN	CARBS	FAT
PLAN A	(1,500)	113G	150G	50G
PLAN B	(1,800)	135G	180G	60G
PLAN C	(2,100)	158G	210G	70G
PLAN D	(2,400)	180G	240G	80G
PLAN E	(2,700)	203G	270G	90G
PLAN F	(3,000)	225G	300G	100G

YOUR PLAN

Write It Here

GOAL 3: Train at least three times per week for a minimum of forty-five minutes. I will discuss the area of fitness in more detail in the next chapter, but for the purposes of highlighting my plan, I wanted to share this here. If your goal is to build muscle, you want to focus on compound body lifts, attempting to increase reps or weight each session. If you have other goals, adjust your activities accordingly. Do simple moves: squats or push-ups. Take into account your athletic hobby here, but remember that forty-five minutes means forty-five minutes of exercise, not forty-five minutes at the gym.

I had a huge wake-up call with this through the use of an Apple Watch that my wife got for me. My watch tells me how physically active I am and how many calories I am actually burning. For example, I found that when playing tennis, singles match play burned twice as many calories as doubles match play. I also found that doing thirty minutes of drills on the court burned more calories than a two-hour singles match did. Make sure you are checking to see that the exercises that you are spending time on are actually achieving the caloric burn that you desire. A simple smart watch like Fitbit, Garmin, or Apple would serve as a shrewd helper in this process to ensure that you are not wasting your time.

Keep in mind that 80 percent of the weight loss is due to goal number one above. All of the rest of it is just gravy. (Mmmm, gravy!)

In addition to the Whole Life plan I've outlined above, here are three lifestyle choices that Taryn and I have found to be helpful as we've implemented these changes in our lives:

1. Stay on the perimeter of the grocery store.

Whole Life eating is focused on eating whole, living foods—things that used to be alive or are currently alive, rather than processed foods. I had never noticed until Taryn pointed it out to me on one of our trips to the grocery store, but most of these items are found in the perimeter of the store. Stay away from the center aisles, where most processed and packaged foods are stored.

2. Watch your portion size.

I used to not even think about the portions I ate. I frequently skipped breakfast and lunch, came home famished, and ate several hamburgers for dinner. I'd then go to sleep on a full stomach. Taryn and I have since learned to eat smaller quantities three to five times a day.

3. Choose food that makes you *feel* good.

Previously I always chose food that tasted good. I was surprised when Taryn told me that her decision about what to eat wasn't primarily based on the taste but instead on how it made her *feel*. Up until that point, I don't think I had ever consciously chosen to eat anything because it would make me feel good. As I made that shift in my thinking, I found that my cravings have changed. I can now sincerely say that food that makes me feel good actually tastes good, too. Back in the day, when I would eat a Big Mac at McDonald's, I felt good for a few seconds, because it tasted so delicious and reminded me of my childhood. But a minute after I ate it, everything would start to slow down. I would feel sluggish and want to take a nap. However, after drinking a protein shake, I feel satisfied and ready to move forward and tackle the rest of my day.

By implementing these nutrition tips, I have maintained my 50-pound weight loss over the past several years and chronic headaches are no longer an issue in my life. In the process, I have also built the muscle mass that I need for the active, on-the-go lifestyle I live. Sometimes I slip up and overeat, but I try to follow the principles of keeping my portions controlled and eating healthily at least 90 percent of the time. I definitely don't deprive myself of the occasional treat, but I don't overeat like I have in the past. Remember, it's all about finding *your* rhythm.

As you make a conscious decision to pursue Whole Life nutrition through eating more whole, living foods, increasing your water intake, and taking supplements, you will be honoring God with your body. By making body health a priority, you are stewarding the incredible gift He has given you!

REVIEW

As the first of three components to body health, nutrition is often the most challenging to change. In this chapter, I shared my personal story of nutrition from my childhood, making major changes in my nutritional intake in the high-intensity phase and moving into nutrition as lifestyle choices.

I also highlighted that changes in nutrition can be broken down into three phases. Those phases include a high-intensity phase, a goal realization phase, and, ultimately, a sustainable Whole Life rhythm phase where your healthy eating plan becomes part of your everyday lifestyle.

To help you live a healthy lifestyle for the long haul, I introduced the need to eat whole, unprocessed foods—including good sources of healthy protein, healthy fats, and carbs, and the need for proper hydration and nutritional supplements. I shared Krista Stryker's "Big Ten" nutrition tips and talked about the three goals that I follow in maintaining proper nutrition, and how to calculate and maintain proper levels of caloric intake for your body.

WHOLE LIFE CHALLENGE

For this chapter's challenge, I encourage you to evaluate where you currently are in the area of nutrition and make a step toward increased body health. As mentioned, I have included a number of links to different nutritional plans in the appendix. Take a look at the plans, consult with your doctor, nutritionist, or dietitian, and pick one that works best for your lifestyle and needs. Pick a start date for the plan, and tell your Whole Life partner, a close friend, or your church small group what you are doing so they can support you.

Since there is no point in having a diet without having a weight goal, write down what you would like to make as a goal for your weight. Give yourself some grace with this goal and break your overall goal down into bite-size goals. This will give you several points of celebration on your weight-loss journey and keep you on the path to ultimate victory.

Along with your new diet, determine the number of glasses of water that you need to drink each day. Use the formula of half your body weight converted to ounces that I shared earlier in this chapter and keep a record of the number of glasses you drink each day to determine how you are doing. You may even want to restock your fridge at home and maybe your car with lots of bottled water as a constant daily reminder.

Find a good multivitamin. I have listed in the appendix the ones that I have developed and use. You can add other nutritional supplements later as you understand your particular body's needs, but, for now, start with a multivitamin. And complete the caloric intake challenge to determine the proper levels of calories, proteins, carbs, and fats you should be eating. Even though this is one of the hardest areas to change, once you take the step, I believe that God will help you succeed and realize your goals as you journey toward your own Whole Life rhythm phase where nutrition is sustained at a healthy level for your optimal productivity and fulfillment.

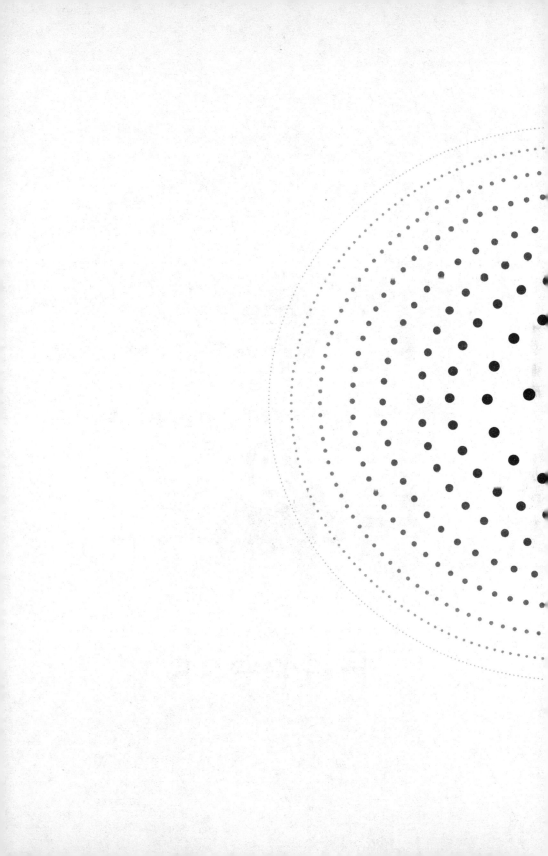

Fitness

nine

Fitness—Decide. Commit. Succeed.

Weight loss doesn't begin in the gym with a
dumb bell; it starts in your head with a decision.
—Toni Sorenson

You have to push past your perceived limits,
push past that point that you thought was as far as you can go.
—Drew Brees

I can do all things through Christ who strengthens me. (NKJV)
—Philippians 4:13

Because I had focused my Christian life only on filling my spirit tank for twenty years, fitness was not even on my radar as something important in my walk with God. If I were to rank myself on the Whole Life Wheel at the beginning of my journey, fitness would have been one of my lowest scores—a 1 or a 2 out of 10 during one of my best weeks.

This was not always the case. In high school, I would have ranked myself an almost perfect 10 in this area. I played tennis five days a week for five to six hours a day. During my senior year of high school, I went to a boarding school for tennis players from around the world. We had an intensely rigorous schedule that was intended to produce the highest-caliber athletes. I was 165 pounds of pure muscle and a force to be reckoned with on the tennis courts, if I do say so myself.

However, my world came crashing down when I tore my ACL in college. After a long twelve-month recovery, I realized I could no longer play competitive tennis, so I decided to take a break from working out. This hiatus lasted about twenty years, broken up by a short stint of pretending to be a runner for a couple of months when I was pursuing Taryn, who was a runner herself. As soon as we officially started dating, I hung up my running shoes. She continued to ask me to go on runs with her until she finally realized my interest in running had only been a desperate attempt to get her to date me.

Twenty years later, my wife was still an avid runner and worked out five days a week. My workouts, by contrast, consisted primarily of wrestling with my kids or running when being chased by a big dog. I made a few unsuccessful attempts to get in shape when I joined a gym, only to have the gym quickly become the place I donated money to every month. I felt like I simply couldn't gain traction in this area, so I gave up.

It was only when I realized that stewarding my body health was an important part of my worship that I gained the motivation I had lacked in previous attempts. First Timothy 4:8 says, "For physical training is of some value, but godliness has value for all things, holding promise for both the present life and the life to come." This passage reinforces that God places the most emphasis on pursuing godliness through spiritual formation, but it also clearly conveys that physical health is also of great importance to the Lord.

In 1 Corinthians 9:24–27 (NKJV), Paul talks about the value in self-discipline, explaining that runners train and compete to get a prize. And that while the earthly runner competes for a temporal crown, we run for an eternal reward as believers in Christ. Paul then says, with that eternal goal in mind, he disciplines his body so he will not be disqualified from the prize. The word translated as *discipline* in 1 Corinthians 9:27 literally means "to strike under the eye" or "to beat black and blue."[1] Paul ensured that his body would be ready at all times so that he would be successful in fulfilling the will of God for his life.

Many people, including believers, allow their bodies to tell their minds what to do, but not athletes. In his article "Living for God's Approval," Keith Krell explains, "The athlete follows the training rules, not his body. He runs when he would rather be resting; he eats a balanced meal when he would rather have a chocolate sundae; he goes to bed when he would rather stay up; and he gets up early to train when he would rather stay in bed. An athlete leads his body; he does not follow it. It is his slave, not the other way around."[2]

Our goal in life should be pursuing God's will, which Paul stresses as spiritual discipline, but he also makes it clear that self-discipline and physical training are important. Remember, if your body tank is empty, it will affect your spirit and soul tanks. If you don't discipline your body, keeping it strong and healthy through exercise and proper nutrition, your body will inevitably start to fall apart, and you may not be physically able to fulfill God's purpose for you in this life. If you are too sick to get out of bed, how can you fulfill your vision for the future? When you feel good physically, it builds your confidence, your passion, and your overall strength and vitality.

When we understand our call as believers to steward our bodies as an act of worship to God, we inherently place more value on the health benefits of physical fitness rather than our outward appearance. I am certainly more comfortable in the slimmer physique I have developed, because I have added physical fitness back into my lifestyle, but the larger benefit has been the increased physical energy, mental clarity, and spiritual alertness that have allowed me to pursue His will for me with greater focus and passion.

HIGH-INTENSITY PHASE

Everything finally aligned for me when I started my road to recovery. After hearing God's message to me about bodily health, I took my physical wellness very seriously. Taryn tried to inspire me years ago by purchasing Tony Horton's P90X, thinking I would be more successful with my workouts if I didn't have to leave the house. P90X is a high-intensity workout program with a ninety-day plan and daily ninety-minute workouts that you can do in your own living room. I tried it a few times, but the commitment required was greater than my motivation level. When P90X3 (the third iteration of the plan) came out, she suggested I might like it better, since the workouts were supposed to be incredibly effective but only thirty minutes long.

I was determined to stay committed this time and see breakthrough in this area. I even took "before" pictures, which were quite embarrassing. I couldn't get the right angle taking selfies in the mirror, so Taryn helped me take the pictures—with both of us laughing at how different I looked from when we first met.

I completed three successive rounds of P90X3, working out six days a week for ninety days each round, and then began a rigorous weight-lifting program afterward. (This was partly motivated by never wanting to have to take embarrassing pictures like that again!) Nine straight months of working out, combined with the traction I gained in eating right, led to a substantial change in my body health. Taryn took another set of pictures nine months after I started working out, which was a much more pleasant experience. I even got a tan, because I was more confident about being out in the sun with my kids without feeling like I had to cover up all the time.

The weight loss, the strength I gained, and the muscle definition I attained were all positive effects, but there was an even greater benefit: an overall boost in energy. The catalytic effects of the improvements in my body health to my spiritual formation and soul care became very apparent to me as I felt more alive and more motivated to grow in every area of my life.

The high-intensity phase in fitness is something like a do-it-yourself version of the classic reality TV show *The Biggest Loser*, where contestants who are in poor health compete to see who can lose the most weight through intense training and nutrition. When they agree to appear on the show, they are committing to make their health and weight a high priority during the weeks of production.

Your high-intensity phase will require that same level of commitment without the benefit of Jillian Michaels breathing down your neck to keep you accountable. If you have neglected regular exercise for years, it will require some major changes to reset your life in this area. If it is unrealistic for you to make it to the gym regularly, try out P90X3, 10 Minute Trainer, YouTube fitness videos, or a DVD-based program you can do in the comfort of your own home in a short amount of time. If you find it difficult to get to the gym or go through the DVD programs by yourself, hire a personal trainer or partner with a friend who will help motivate you and keep you accountable.

The biggest mistake people make when they are trying to get in shape is expecting too much too soon. When they don't see as much change as they were hoping for in their ideal timeframe, they quit. It's like that famous tortoise-and-hare story, where the slow-and-steady tortoise wins the race. In your pursuit of physical health, be the tortoise and you will eventually succeed.

When you are sick, take a break, but try to be as consistent as possible. If you don't want to spread your germs at the gym, do some physical activity at home until your health returns. When you are injured, work out any area that is not injured, and be very careful with the hurt area.

If weight loss is your goal, this will be the hardest but the most important phase. I lost between 35 and 40 pounds during this intense phase. You will need to push yourself to go to the gym when you would rather stay in bed. Some days it will feel uncomfortable and your muscles will hurt. But if you stick to your high-intensity plan, you will experience results.

GOAL REALIZATION PHASE

The high-intensity phase is not sustainable forever, and after three to six months you will be able to transition to a routine that is more realistic for the long term. Hopefully your transition will be smoother than mine. During my high-intensity P90X3 program and weight-lifting regime, I discovered I had arthritis in my shoulder. I was overly ambitious, picturing myself competing in bodybuilding competitions, which quickly led to unrealistic expectations of what I could do. I decided to go for broke, and my body ended up breaking in the process. The result was a minor surgery that set me back a couple of months. The worst part of the surgery is that I had it only a few days after turning forty. Talk about making me feel old! Looking back, I think the surgery may have fueled my fire to get fit even more.

In the goal realization phase, you will begin to find out what is sustainable for you. After my shoulder surgery, I continued with the P90X3 trainings three to six days a week but gradually moved over to the gym, focusing on a different part of the body or different exercise machine on each visit. I tried running for six months until I hurt my knee and realized that was not for me. I then rediscovered tennis. For many of us, we had an athletic hobby that we enjoyed during a younger season in our lives: basketball, tennis, soccer, etc. Although I no longer have hopes of becoming a tennis champion, I've loved picking it back up as recreation and great exercise. It was in this phase that I achieved my goal weight of 185 pounds.

WHOLE LIFE RHYTHM PHASE

You'll know you are in the Whole Life rhythm phase when you are regularly reaching and maintaining your fitness goals and your physical activities are a normal part of your routine. For me, I felt I had reached this phase when I reached my weight goal and adopted the additional fitness lifestyle changes as part of my weekly rhythm. Your body tank will no longer drain energy from your spirit and soul tanks. In fact, your newfound physical health and stamina will have positively affected your spirit and soul, increasing your clarity and focus to pursue your dream.

I now work out at the gym three days a week and have integrated what I call my athletic hobby—tennis—into my lifestyle. My physical activities have become a fixture on my calendar, and I actually enjoy my weekly tennis nights enough that I would never consider missing them. I now set annual goals for my fitness and weight and keep myself accountable to hit these benchmarks by maintaining my fitness program in my Whole Life rhythm. It has been in this phase that I achieved my new goal of maintaining my end of college weight of 175 pounds.

Tony Horton shared some of his thoughts with me on the flexibility and enjoyment that should be a part of your Whole Life rhythm phase. Regardless of the fitness plan you use, these points are practical and foundational, and will benefit you in whatever phase you find yourself.

- ✦ **Be realistic in what you do.** Based on your age, current physical condition, and body type, choose workouts that are realistic as far as what you can and should do. What was appropriate for you at a certain age or life stage may not work for you today.

- ✦ **Find workouts that you will enjoy.** Try combining a variety of sports, like tennis or basketball, with exercises and workouts. Variety will keep you from getting bored, and doing things you enjoy will keep you coming back for more.

- ✦ **Explore the options.** Most communities sponsor athletic competitions, races, and/or classes at the local YMCA or junior colleges. Using a goal of running in a local race or competing in some other sport can be great motivation to get you moving toward your fitness goals.

Tennis tournaments have been great motivation for me. Activities, competitions, and classes are available year-round, both indoors and outdoors. Taryn has done classes of all sorts through the years including barre, spin, and Pilates, and has consistently participated in pay-per-class workouts held in many of today's boutique gyms, like Orangetheory Fitness and Solidcore.

✦ **Use your calendar to keep yourself accountable.** My tennis nights vary each week, depending upon who and when I can play, but I maintain my practice at least three nights a week, after the kids are off to bed, early in the morning, or even on my lunch hour. These time slots work best, since I can still be with my family at night and have time to walk and pray with Taryn before going to bed. Putting these times in my calendar forces me to consistently make room for workouts and tennis times in my schedule while also keeping family and social relationships as a priority.

I DON'T HAVE THE TIME!

Have you repeated those words to others or allowed them to pass through your mind as you considered adding fitness to your lifestyle? After avoiding physical training for almost twenty years, this was one of my excuses for not getting back to the gym. Remember, Taryn tried to get me interested in Tony Horton's P90X, which was too much of a time commitment for me in that season of my life (ninety whole minutes!). Later, when the P90X3 program came out, I had no excuses. The thirty-minute workouts were short enough that I could definitely add them to my busy schedule.

Many people that I have talked to—both those who attended my church and personal friends outside the church—had battles prioritizing exercise and setting aside enough time for it in their busy lives. Some have come up with creative ways to reprioritize their lives to include exercise. When my wife had our third child, the demands on her life went up tremendously. Since she was determined to make it work, she got up at five a.m., drove to the gym, worked out for an hour, then headed home to feed the baby and get the kids off to school. She has also had seasons when she has done videos at home or gone to the gym at creative times of the day and night. There was even a period where I built her a gym in our basement! If you decide to make fitness a priority, you will find a way to make it happen, possibly even cutting back on TV or social media to find that extra time.

If your excuse for not working on the area of fitness in your Whole Life journey is that you don't have the time, I have another option for you. Perhaps you don't have an hour a day or even thirty minutes a day to exercise, but do you have twelve minutes, three times a week?

High-intensity interval training (HIIT) is the foundation for a twelve-minute workout concept created by Krista Stryker. As a personal trainer in New York City, Krista worked out for hours each day, diligently doing cardio, weight training, and sports-specific training every day until she was overtrained, injured, and had little time in her day for anything else. When she discovered HIIT training, it turned everything she knew about fitness and exercise upside down.

HIIT is an advanced form of interval training and an exercise strategy that alternates periods of short, intense anaerobic exercise with less intense recovery periods. As Krista told me, that basically means you'll be working as hard as humanly possible for a short amount of time, resting, then working hard again. The great part is that an entire HIIT session usually only lasts for about ten to twenty minutes. It's an incredibly efficient way of training that produces results quickly. The 12 Minute Athlete workouts are easy to fit into your day. Everyone has an extra twelve minutes.

Krista recommends HIIT workouts three times a week, so I asked her to create three Whole Life HIIT workouts for beginner, intermediate, and advanced levels. These workouts will give you a sampling of HIIT workouts, and if you want to continue, there are a wide variety of workouts available on her website and the 12 Minute Athlete app, with demonstrations of each exercise. (Check out the link to her app in the appendix.)

HIIT 12 MINUTE WORKOUTS

General Instructions: Set an interval timer for eighteen rounds of ten-second and thirty-second intervals. Rest on the ten-second intervals, then work as hard as you possibly can on the thirty-second intervals. Follow the order of the exercises (one exercise per thirty-second interval) until the timer beeps. If you are unfamiliar with the names of these workouts, a good way to learn them is to look up videos of them online in order to ensure you are using the proper posture to maximize each workout.

Whole Life HIIT workout for someone who is a beginner.

Beginner Set #1: 1. Burpees; 2. Air squats; 3. High knees; 4. Snowboarder jumps; 5. Push-ups; 6. Sit-ups.

Beginner Set #2: 1. Squat jumps; 2. Reptile push-ups; 3. High knees; 4. Step-ups; 5. Speed skater lunges; 6. Mountain climbers.

Beginner Set #3: 1. High knees; 2. Air squats; 3. Burpees; 4. Step-ups; 5. Mountain climbers; 6. Sit-ups.

Whole Life HIIT workout for someone who is intermediate.

Intermediate Set #1: 1. Burpee tuck jumps; 2. Side lunges; 3. Burpee lateral jumps; 4. Air squats; 5. High knees; 6. Split-leg V-ups.

Intermediate Set #2: 1. Snowboarder jumps; 2. Push-up plank jumps; 3. Jump lunges; 4. Pike jumps; 5. High knees; 6. Plank get-ups.

Intermediate Set #3: 1. Squat jumps; 2. Push-ups; 3. Burpee lateral jumps; 4. Side lunges; 5. Tuck jumps; 6. V-ups.

Whole Life HIIT workout for someone who is advanced.

Advanced Set #1: 1. Jump lunge squat combo; 2. Diamond push-ups; 3. Pistol squats; 4. Burpees; 5. Pike jumps; 6. Split-leg V-ups.

Advanced Set #2: 1. Burpee pull-ups; 2. Handstand push-ups; 3. High knees; 4. Pistol squats; 5. Chin-ups; 6. Hanging leg raises.

Advanced Set #3: 1. Long jumps; 2. Traveling reptile push-ups; 3. Line sprints; 4. Burpee lateral jumps; 5. Jump lunges; 6. V-ups.

There is also a workout called the Scientific 7-Minute Workout with an accompanying app. Scientists at McMaster University in Hamilton, Ontario, and other institutions have concluded that even a few minutes of training at an intensity approaching your maximum capacity produces molecular changes within muscles comparable to those of several hours of running or bike riding.

This workout involves simple exercises that should be performed in rapid succession, allowing thirty seconds for each, while throughout the intensity hovers at about an 8 on a discomfort scale of about 10. One doctor even *recommends* that those seven minutes should be unpleasant. The upside is obvious: After seven minutes, you're done.[3]

THE BENEFITS OF WEIGHT TRAINING AND AEROBIC AND ANAEROBIC EXERCISE

Aerobic exercise, weight training, and anaerobic exercise each have specific benefits. Aerobic exercises are sustained exercises such as jogging, rowing, swimming, or cycling. They stimulate and strengthen the heart and lungs and improve the body's use of oxygen. Weight training uses resistance to make your muscles work and build strength. Anaerobic exercise (Krysta's plan) is intense enough to promote strength, speed, and power.

Focusing mainly on **aerobic exercise**:

1. Increases your confidence, emotional stability, memory, and brain function.

2. Strengthens your heart and lungs, lowers your cholesterol and risk of type 2 diabetes, improves immune function, and lowers blood pressure.

3. Burns up calories, which can help you to shed excess weight.

4. Tones muscles and improves posture.

5. Increases stamina, giving you more energy for both work and play. You will sleep better, handle stress better, and feel better about yourself.[4]

Adding **weight training** to your aerobic training:

1. Increases your physical workout capacity and improves your ability to perform activities in daily life.

2. Improves bone density.

3. Promotes fat-free body mass.

4. Increases the strength of connective tissue, muscles, and tendons, improving motor performance and decreasing injury risk.

5. Improves your life quality as you gain body confidence.[5]

Although it does not burn as many calories as aerobic exercise and is less important in cardiovascular fitness, **anaerobic exercise**:

1. Is much better at building overall strength and muscle mass.

2. Increases the maximum amount of oxygen you use during exercise, improving your cardio and respiratory fitness.

3. Increases your endurance and the ability to stand fatigue.

4. Helps with weight loss because building muscles takes a lot of energy.

5. Boosts metabolism through increased lean muscle mass, again helping with weight loss and decreasing body fat.[6]

GET SUPPORT

I believe that, like most things in life, fitness is more fun when it is not done alone. I recommend working out with a partner. Having a fitness partner will keep you accountable and ensure a higher success rate. If you choose a solo workout, at least have your Whole Life partner checking in on your progress. My wife even has a workout buddy in a different city, but they use the activity app on their Apple Watches to get progress updates on each other and send encouraging messages when they complete a workout. A study done at Stanford University found that simply receiving a check-in phone call asking about your progress every two weeks increased the amount of exercise participants did by an average 78 percent.[7]

Some of my best seasons of working out have included a workout partner. The biggest lift was the accountability: There is nothing quite like knowing the other person is waiting at the gym for you to keep you consistent. Here are several different types of workouts that all require someone else to work out with you.

1. Friend Trainer

If you can find a friend whose schedule complements yours, coordinate your workouts together for a time that works best for you both. I have been more successful when I have had a workout buddy because of the accountability. The Department of Kinesiology at the School of Public Health, Indiana University, Bloomington, found that couples who worked out separately had a 43 percent dropout rate, while those who went to the gym together had only a 6.3 percent dropout rate.[8] Maybe you and your Whole Life partner can even work out together!

2. Personal Trainer

This is a great option if you have the financial resources to invest in a personal trainer. Not only do they provide accountability, they are trained to design your workouts to cater to your strengths, weaknesses, and personal goals, and work with you to correct your form. Your local gym is a great place to find a personal trainer. If you can find a friend who has a similar schedule, consider going together and splitting the cost. Taryn and I have both used a personal trainer to recover from an injury or to reach specific goals. If you're tight on funds, many gyms allow you to test their personal training out with a complimentary session, during which you can ask for three to five workouts you can do over the next several months to reach your individual goal.

3. Video or App Trainer

This has been my favorite option in the past because it is so convenient. I can press "play" whenever I want, and Tony Horton becomes my personal trainer via video. If you have a friend who is experienced in fitness, or you can afford a few sessions of personal training, consider inviting them over when you are going through the different videos to check your form. Unfortunately, your video or app trainer can't hold you accountable, so you will need to tell your Whole Life partner your plan and allow him or her to provide accountability.

If Christ is in your life, your body is a temple of the Holy Spirit that dwells in you. As you steward your body and experience the many benefits of physical fitness—increased strength and energy, slimmer and toned physique, and improved health—you will be better able to accomplish your clarified dream and the purpose that He has for your life.

REVIEW

As we looked at the role of fitness in living a whole life, I talked about the three phases you will pass through to arrive at a rhythm for your life. First is the high-intensity phase where you are introducing major changes in your life to counteract years of neglect. Second is the goal realization phase, where you move to routines that are realistic and sustainable for the long term. Third is the Whole Life rhythm phase, where your fitness routine and activities are a consistent part of your life and help you maintain your fitness goals.

We addressed the often-given excuse of no time to exercise by introducing Krista Stryker's high-intensity interval training (HIIT), the 12 Minute Athlete, and the Scientific 7-minute Workout.

We ended the chapter comparing the benefits of aerobic exercise, weight training, and anaerobic exercise, and my strong suggestion to find a friend or personal trainer to help you stick with and achieve your fitness goals.

WHOLE LIFE CHALLENGE

So, where are you in your Whole Life journey in the area of fitness? Do you need a season of high intensity to get your body into shape after years of neglect like I did? Do you need to set goals to make fitness a sustainable part of your life?

The information in this chapter won't do anything for you unless you set goals and commit to a plan. At the beginning of all of Tony Horton's training videos, they have a slogan I love: "Decide. Commit. Succeed."[9] To make the needed changes to move you toward a Whole Life rhythm in the area of fitness, I encourage you to do the following:

1. Decide.

What are your fitness goals? Would you like to lose weight? How much? Do you want to become more muscular and toned? Do you have a specific achievement to reach, like running a mile in under ten minutes or competing in a competition? Take some time to think about your fitness goals and write them down in your journal.

2. Commit.

What is your fitness plan? What workout(s) are you going to do and when will you fit them in? If you have a busy and often overbooked schedule, I challenge you to commit to workouts and schedule them in your calendar at least three days per week to start. Write down the fitness plan that you have decided upon in your journal. Also, write down an event in the future to have as a goal to attend, like going to the beach or running in a race. These events will help you to stay committed and on track with your goal.

3. Succeed.

I am confident that if you commit to working out three days a week, you will experience positive results in your body health. Armed with the knowledge that you are stewarding the body God has given you, He will empower you to keep up your regimen to develop the strength, health, and energy to accomplish all that He calls you to do in this life.

Rest

ten

Rest—Recreate, Recharge, and Refocus

Early to bed and early to rise,
makes a man healthy, wealthy and wise.
—Benjamin Franklin

O sleep, O gentle sleep,
Nature's soft nurse, how have I frighted thee,
That thou no more wilt weigh my eyelids down,
And steep my senses in forgetfulness?
—William Shakespeare, *Henry IV*, Part II, Act III, Scene I

The Lord is my shepherd, I shall not want. He makes me lie
down in green pastures; He leads me beside quiet waters.
—Psalm 23:1–2[1]

As a strong type A personality working in a high-energy, multisite ministry, rest was something that God had to make me pay attention to. I was like the sheep in Psalm 23 who did not want to voluntarily lie down. The shepherd knows his sheep cannot be in perpetual motion without burning out. Unfortunately, the sheep don't have the sense to know when to stop, and the shepherd has to *make* them lie down. God has designed us like the sheep and knows there are times when we need to stop and rest.

In our go-go-go society, it's often hard to convince ourselves that we need to stop and rest. Any pause in our schedules seems to open us up to the fear that we will end up with less than our neighbors or not succeed in our chosen careers. Adding to that fear, the enemy encourages us to keep pushing ahead in our busy schedules, even when we are exhausted, by keeping the focus of our lives on our efforts instead of God's provision. Ultimately, if our trust is in Him, we can slow down our lives for a Sabbath rest, believing He will take care of our affairs for one day while we recharge.

It took me years before my stubbornness gave way and I saw the importance in resting. Rest made it into the Ten Commandments, which was a pretty good indication that I needed to integrate it into my Whole Life rhythm. God has another way for us to live, so be encouraged that you can achieve a work-life balance that is in sync with His calling.

If you are a workaholic like I was, don't worry. Rest will become a part of your new Whole Life rhythm when you understand how it fits into God's plan for your life. In Exodus chapter 20, God shares the Ten Commandments with Moses. The fourth of the ten is: "Remember the Sabbath day by keeping it Holy. Six days you shall labor and do all your work, but the seventh day is a Sabbath to the Lord your God" (Exodus 20:8–10).

Our Creator understands our design and knows that if we don't rest, we will eventually burn out and function incorrectly. Psalm 127:2 says, "It is useless for you to work so hard from early morning until late at night, anxiously working for food to eat; for God gives rest to his loved ones."[2] While work is something that God wants us to prioritize in our lives, God knows the importance of rest and wants to give us the time and space needed to recharge.

The importance God has placed on our periods of recuperation is best represented by the commonly-used acronym REST and helps explain how rest refocuses us for the active parts of life.

R-E-S-T

R = Realize Your Worth

The Bible has a lot to say about our worth. James 1:18 says, "God decided to give us life through the word of truth so we might be the most important of all the things he made."[3] Matthew 6:26 tells us to look at the birds who don't sow or reap, but who are still provided for by our heavenly Father every day. Matthew then compares our worth to that of the birds, "And aren't you far more valuable to him than they are?" Whenever we look at humanity—or our individual lives—from God's perspective, we find that we are way more valuable to Him than we ever considered.

In Isaiah 49:16, God says, "See, I have engraved you on the palms of my hands." Jesus has a tattoo of your name on the hands that were pierced for you. This is said in Scripture to remind you that He has a very high value for you. When you understand how much you are valued by our heavenly Father, you begin to understand that you are more than what society tells you about yourself, and more than you give yourself credit for before God.

Having a work life that is out of balance can be commonplace—even encouraged and affirmed—in some parts of our society. Sometimes the heavy workload is unavoidable if you are a stay-at-home mom with multiple children, or a caregiver, or work multiple jobs to meet your basic needs. But other times it is driven by an issue of identity. It is important to realize that your worth is not in your work alone. After initially moving to the D.C. area, I realized that every conversation with strangers followed a predictable pattern. People didn't start a conversation by asking "What is your name?" or "Where are you from?" but rather "What do you do?"

Our society often assumes that our value is wrapped up in how successful we are, what our titles are, or how much money we make. If your value and identity is in what you do, then if you are doing something successfully, you'll feel good about your identity. But on your bad days, when you are not doing well, you feel bad about who you are. God never intended your identity to be about what you do. He intends your identity to be based on your relationship to Him as a precious son or daughter.

R-E-S-T

E = Enjoy What You Have Already Worked For

Ecclesiastes 4:4 says, "Then I saw that all toil and all skill in work come from a man's envy of his neighbor."[4] This tells us that one reason we can be driven to work so hard is to impress others. Here in the United States, we call that keeping up with the Joneses. We all know the ubiquitous "Jones" family that lives right next door to us. When the Joneses get a new car, *we* need a new car. If the Joneses get the latest TV, *we* all of the sudden need the latest TV. Dave Ramsey said in his book, *Total Money Makeover: A Proven Plan for Financial Fitness*,[5] "We buy things we don't need with money we don't have in order to impress people we don't like." It is crazy to me how true that can be.

God has a different system than keeping up with the Joneses. It's called enjoying what you already have. Ecclesiastes 3:13 says, "God wants all people to eat and drink and be happy in their work, which are gifts from God."[6]

In the beginning of creation, God worked very hard creating the heavens and the earth, the sea, the land, and everything within. He created the fish in the water and the birds in the sky. He created the land animals. Then He created humanity. Nonetheless, He worked only six days. At the end of day six, "God saw all that he had made, and it was very good. And there was evening, and there was morning—the sixth day" (Genesis 1:31). God seemed to turn around and look back over the prior six days of work and after a moment of reflection He says, "It was very good" (Genesis 1:31). God was basically complimenting Himself. He took a step back just to see how much He had accomplished and how good His work was.

Genesis 2:1–3 says, "Thus the heavens and the earth were completed in all their vast array. By the seventh day God had finished the work he had been doing; so on the seventh day He rested from all his work. Then God blessed the seventh day and made it holy, because on it He rested from all the work of creating that he had done." If God can take a step back, compliment Himself on all He has accomplished, and take a day to rest, we who have far less responsibility and power should be able to do the same.

For God, the Sabbath was a day set apart from work. This has helped me understand that the Sabbath is a day for us to enjoy what we have already worked for. It is a day to look back and observe and see how good those six days really were. We often think it's a day to do nothing, but I think it's the day God chose to stop creating and instead focus on recreating. It is a day for us to do something other than work. Instead of create, we recreate.

This notion has helped me understand what the Psalmist meant when he said, "The Lord is my shepherd, I shall not want" (Psalm 23:1).[7] Oftentimes, when I got to my day of rest, I became anxious thinking about all that was on my to-do list and pondering why I was not doing more. But at some point I understood that even God had to stop and look back over His work and actually say, "You know what, this was very good." That understanding helps me to enjoy what I have already worked for and where I have already been. I'm not a huge proponent of *looking back* in regretful ways, but I do like looking back in thankful ways. I've learned to use it to get myself excited for the road ahead.

R-E-**S**-T

S = Stop Striving and Start Trusting

As an individual who strove often, I found the antidote was in the very thing that I was ignoring in my life. I was pushing hard because

I wasn't practicing a key to the Christian life. When we strive, we actually believe that our successes are because of our own efforts. The opposite-of-strivings antidote is faith or trust. Proverbs 3:5–6 says, "Trust in the Lord with all your heart, and do not lean on your own understanding. In all your ways acknowledge Him, and He will make your paths straight."[8] Trust takes the emphasis off of my striving and puts the emphasis back on His direction. When we trust in God's plan and the importance He has placed on rest, we find that it alleviates stress and strengthens our faith.

Because God took a break from His work, you can stop and take a break as well. Hebrews 4:9–11 says, "There remains, then, a Sabbath-rest for the people of God; for anyone who enters God's rest also rests from their works, just as God did from his. Let us, therefore, make every effort to enter that rest, so that no one will perish by following their example of disobedience."

The title on Hebrews chapter 4 in my Bible is "A Sabbath Rest for God's People." I believe God is saying, "Look, I am going to give you six days when you can advance your livelihood through work. But on the seventh day, I need you to be full of faith and understand that I am going to watch over whatever you have been entrusted to watch over. I need you to rest on this day so you can continue to accomplish great things in the next six days. Then I need you to trust me again because this cycle is going to continue every single week."

Taking a day of rest is actually an act of trust. The Bible says in Hebrews 4:3 that faith is the way that we accept Sabbath rest into our lives. The only time the Bible tells us to strive is in Hebrews 4:11: "Let us therefore *strive to enter that rest*, so that no one may fall by the same sort of disobedience."[9] It tells us to not strive for anything except to rest. God needs you to strive to enter into the rest, so that you will not fall under disobedience. I think this type of faith is best expressed by having a day set aside to go to church, spend quality time with friends and family, and do something that will recharge your spirit, soul, and body.

Disobedience is doubt, the opposite of faith and trust. We must strive to enter our day of rest—the one day that we have to set things aside that we would normally take home and work on. Trusting God on the Sabbath not only provides rest for our bodies; it also refreshes our souls and spirits as we reflect on God's goodness in our lives over the prior week and receive new strength and direction for the week ahead.

R-E-S-T

T = Transfer Life's Pressures to God's Ability

We have so many things that we can be anxious and stressed about in our lives. Jesus gives us the solution for this in Matthew 11:28–30, right before He starts talking about the Sabbath. He says, "Come to me, all you who are weary and burdened, and I will give you rest. Take my yoke upon you and learn from me, for I am gentle and humble in heart, and you will find rest for your souls. For my yoke is easy and my burden is light."

In biblical times, the yoke was a large wooden object that rested on the necks of a pair of oxen. When attached to a cart or farm equipment, the oxen worked together, combining their strength to get the needed task done. When we bring our heavy burdens and exhaustion to Jesus and take on His yoke, He carries those burdens. In exchange, we are promised rest for our souls.

If the two oxen yoked together were unequal in strength or height, they were unable to do what the farmer needed. Jesus is not stressed or anxious, but we are. It sounds like we are unequal for the task. That's why He invites us to learn from Him. Let Him teach you how to rely on His strength, to trust in His ability to work in and through you. The yoke you have been trying to carry by yourself has been heavy, but His is easy. When you let Jesus carry your burden, it becomes light.

Use your Sabbath to transfer your heavy burden. Whatever you are dealing with, whatever you are distressed about, give pressure points for the week to Him. If it helps, make a list of your pressure points and visualize physically handing them over to Him. Jesus does not feel pressure about anything that you are experiencing. He is way bigger than even your biggest issue; because He loves you, He is going to take care of those things you hand over to Him.

Jesus said, "The Sabbath was made for man, not man for the Sabbath" (Mark 2:27). The Sabbath is not meant as a religious duty, a punishment, or burden on your life. It was especially created as a blessing for everyone. The focus of the day should not be on what you are giving up or the extra hours that you could be working. If you don't stop, take a pause, and freely receive His mercy for one day, you are not going to make it through the next six days and do all that He wants or needs you to do.

When I was a kid we used to wrestle and play king of the hill. Occasionally there was something called the mercy rule. In the middle of the conquest or fight, when you needed a break you said "Uncle" or "Mercy." If your opponents were playing fair, they gave you a break to catch your breath so you could jump back into the fight. God knew that you and I were going to need a moment to catch our breaths every seven days. Before we could even call mercy, He wanted us to know that taking a day off would not be a sacrifice for us. The Sabbath is God calling "Mercy" for you. Enjoy it, because rest is God's way of taking care of us.

THREE KEYS TO REST ON THE SABBATH

When I talk about a Sabbath rest, many people tell me how hard it is to take a day for rest. Even those who attend church on Sunday can find the day anything but restful. The three keys I share below will give you some specific ideas about things you can do to cultivate your spirit, soul, and body on your Sabbath.

1. The first key to rest is your physical body.

When my body doesn't get sufficient rest, I get cranky. If we're being honest, I'm sure you do, too. Dictionary.com defines rest as "Refreshing ease or inactivity after exertion or labor."[10] When we rest, we take it easy or slow our pace down from our prior activities.

Rest can also be recreation—re-creating energy. If the thing that recharges and refreshes you is recreation, do some on your Sabbath. If you recharge by being around other people, I encourage you to do that. Do something different than your other workdays: Change the pace and the activities. Do the thing that recharges you and rests your body.

2. The second key to rest is to recharge your soul.

When your soul is tired, it affects your perspective on life (your mind), your emotions begin to take charge and drag you on a roller-coaster ride—up one minute and down the next—and you can make bad decisions (your will).

Recharging your soul involves self-care activities, like reading a book, taking a long, hot bath, or walking outside in nature. Do something that you like to do—a special activity that doesn't make it into your regular routine.

Mark 8:36 says, "What good is it for someone to gain the whole world, yet forfeit their soul?" In other words, if you continue to be on the go without ever resting, you'll never have a reset for your soul. As your soul rests, it will help you reset and realign your focus on God, and your spirit.

3. The third key to rest is to refocus your spirit.

A significant part of celebrating the Sabbath the way that God designed is by being in the house of God. David went to the temple for His Sabbath. Jesus went to the temple. Attending church is like hitting the reset button on your spirit.

If you are not able to attend services on Saturday or Sunday, take some special time on your Sabbath for prayer. Refocus your spirit by talking to God, opening up the lines of communication with Him. Remember that communicating with God is two-way conversation. You speak to Him but you also need to let Him talk to you. Communication can be as simple as journaling a letter to Him and allowing Him to speak back to you as you write what you believe He is saying to you.

Some people like to walk and pray. There is something about being outside in nature on a beautiful day that is calming and refocuses their souls and spirits. Others will have an extended devotional time with Him. When the calendar is free of work appointments, there is extra time to spend on the Bible or in an open-ended time of prayer.

WHAT HAPPENS WHEN WE DON'T REST?

Israel was commanded to set aside the seventh year of each agricultural cycle in order for the land to receive a Sabbath rest (see Leviticus 25:1–7). God warned Israel about the punishments that would follow if this commandment was not obeyed (see Leviticus 26:27–46). For 490 consecutive years, Israel never let the land have a Sabbath year's rest. This came to a total of seventy missed Sabbath years of rest for the land. As a result of this specific disobedience, God allowed Israel to be taken captive for a period of seventy years (see 2 Chronicles 36:21). This period of time equaled one year of captivity for each of the missed Sabbath years.[11] That's how important God's rest is to our lives! Clearly this whole ordeal happened under the old covenant captured in the Old Testament.

Now, because of the New Testament Covenant we have in Christ, we may not be physically taken captive by our lack of rest. However, over time, we likely will find that denying ourselves rest will not be followed by the blessings of a whole life. I personally tried to ignore this area of the whole life for years. My work-life balance was out of rhythm, and I based my self-worth entirely on my performance. Acting like my success was solely based on my effort, I spent an inordinate amount of time and energy focused on work, ignoring the health of my soul, body, and even to some extent, my family.

As my ungodly beliefs about self were replaced by godly beliefs, I have realized that when I obey and take a Sabbath rest, my trust is in Him and His ability more than in my ability to perform and make things happen. Now that I have experienced the blessings of taking regular rest and the intent behind God's command to take a Sabbath, it has become a nonnegotiable in my life, and I am extremely grateful for them and the heightened faith and trust that they bring.

THE RHYTHMS OF REST

As we work toward restoring our bodily health, I want to outline the different rhythms and seasons of rest God has intended for our lives in addition to observing the Sabbath.

Daily rest: Humans spend up to one-third of our lives sleeping. The National Sleep Foundation recommends that most adults get anywhere from seven to nine hours of sleep a night. They actually recommend that you make sleep a priority, not just an afterthought after you finish all your other tasks in life.[12] The quality of your hours spent awake—your energy level, concentration, and productivity—are often linked to giving yourself the sleep you need. As you know, at the height of my burnout and undiagnosed Graves' disease, I was sleeping about two hours a night. This was clearly unsustainable, but it had gone on this way for at least a year or more. Learning about the priority of daily rest and the science behind it propelled me to talk to my doctor about this area as well. This led to some very simple and effective solutions.

Some things that helped to make sleep a priority included sticking to a consistent bedtime schedule. This includes going to bed at the same time every night (even on the weekends), having a relaxation routine before bed to help you wind down (think hot herbal tea and a good book), and making sure your room and bed are conducive to a sound night's sleep—no bright lights, lumpy mattresses, or electronic devices in your face too close to bedtime. There is actually something called blue light, which is emitted from your iPhone or tablet. When you spend time with your electronic device before bed, the blue light fools your brain into thinking it's still daytime. If you have tried all my suggestions and still have difficulty sleeping, I highly recommend scheduling an appointment with your doctor to discuss what simple solutions may work for you.

Weekly rest: Your weekly rest is called the Sabbath. Traditionally it's ideal to take your Sabbath on a Saturday or Sunday so you can include church attendance in your day, but if you have to work those days, try to find something that best fits your lifestyle. Don't let the day of the week—or necessary responsibilities like feeding the dog, changing diapers, paying bills, or making lunch—detract from the purpose of a Sabbath: to connect with God and let Him refresh you.

A great way to approach your Sabbath is by thinking of things you can do to draw closer to God instead of what you have to give up so the day qualifies as "the Sabbath." In the Spirit section of this book, I mentioned some activities, such as an extended devotional time, that build your relationship with Him and refresh you spiritually. Beyond church and a time with Him, make space for other activities that you enjoy and refresh you, such as hobbies or sports.

This area was a big challenge for me. As I have committed to a Sabbath in my week, God has helped me finish everything I need to do each week. I've learned to better plan ahead to get things done on time, and He's shown me that some things I thought were a priority can often wait for another day or week. After experiencing a couple major burnouts, my priorities began to change, and I understood the need for routine rest. I was the overambitious type, with a long list of work-related to-dos that could never be accomplished. I've pared back, gotten my priorities back in place, and trust God to take care of the things I can't accomplish. Understanding and experiencing the Sabbath as part of my weekly rhythm has definitely helped me in my quest to live a whole life.

Quarterly rest: In addition to daily and weekly rest, I've also recognized the importance of integrating a quarterly rest into my schedule. Most quarters, Taryn and I get away for an overnight retreat (or a couple days when possible). But on many occasions, like when we can't get a babysitter, or another circumstance arises, we simply plan a day that we spend together while the kids participate in other activities. I use my quarterly rest to have an extended time to connect with God: time in prayer, two-way journaling, and assessing where I am with my current dreams and goals. It really helps to have a change of scenery to meet God and honestly evaluate my soul. I also pull out my Whole Life Wheel to make sure I am continuing to operate smoothly in all areas.

Along with ample prayer time and personal reflection, I try to do something fun or relaxing, like fishing or family time. When Taryn joins me, we do something we both enjoy, like searching antique shops for unique items, looking at houses, taking a hike, or going on a scenic drive together. The simple idea of retreat is to come off the front lines so that you can reflect, recover, and return with renewed passion for your assignment called life.

THE THREE PHASES OF REST

As I grew in my experience of rest, I realized that I went through the same three phases that I experienced for nutrition and fitness: high intensity, goal realization, and the Whole Life rhythm phase. The high-intensity phase of rest took place during the extended burnout and sickness recovery I mentioned at the beginning of the book. I was in terrible shape in all areas of my life, and a drastic change was needed to steer me away from the burnout I was experiencing. Some of you may be in a similar place, where you need a major break to jump-start significant changes in your life.

For many people, this type of reset is necessary after a major life transition: losing a job, ending a relationship or marriage, the death of a loved one, or recovering from a major life trauma. Before you press ahead into the next season in life, it is important to detox from the last. Since the spirit, soul, and body are interconnected, mental or emotional trauma will affect your body and spirit and keep you from moving forward in life with confidence.

There are ministries and retreat centers that focus on the needs of those requiring this type of rest. Often situated amid natural beauty, they offer accommodations for you to rest and reflect, often with a counselor to help you process your thoughts and feelings. An acquaintance of mine spent three weeks in a retreat house in the mountains of Virginia after losing his job. The isolation and beauty of the location combined with the listening ears of counselors helped his body find rest, his spirit find refreshment, and his mind find a fresh focus for the future.

Unfortunately, the high-intensity phase is not sustainable as a lifestyle. Most of us do not have the time or money to take an extended break each year. Also, we don't need the major reset that takes place in the high-intensity phase every year. We need to develop patterns of rest that fit with our Whole Life lifestyle. The goal realization phase is where we develop patterns of rest that work with a sustainable lifestyle so we can achieve a Whole Life rhythm.

If you are not able to do the extended study retreat every year, incorporate quarterly weekend retreats, like I mentioned earlier. I also plan a weekly Sabbath day when I focus on activities that recharge me physically, emotionally, and spiritually. Since I am a pastor, Saturdays and Sundays are often busy workdays for me where I am often ministering and traveling to speak at different churches, so I plan my Sabbath days on Mondays or even Tuesdays, depending on my travel schedule. If you are not working a job that requires you to work on the weekend, try to take your Sabbath on Saturday or Sunday so you can include worship. I also make sure I am getting adequate sleep each night and carve out time each morning to work on my spirit, soul, and body through exercise at the gym and time with the Lord.

I've learned to set better boundaries in my life in order to keep my rest periods sacred, which has in turn led to better productivity in my work life and more quality time with family and friends. As I have experienced the benefits of rest, He has healed me from some of the ungodly beliefs that were feeding my workaholic nature, and I can now set aside a day each week for a Sabbath, trusting that God will bless my obedience by blessing my work during the other six days. I now recognize the purpose that God intended for rest and make it a priority to keep me in a Whole Life rhythm.

REVIEW

As the third component in your body health, rest is much needed but often ignored. In this chapter, we learned the commonly used acronym REST. As we realize our worth to God (R), enjoy what we have already worked for (E), stop striving and start trusting (S), and transfer life's pressures to God's ability (T), we position ourselves to receive the rest God has for us.

We studied the three keys to rest on the Sabbath: resting your physical body, recharging your soul, and refocusing your spirit. And, from Israel's Old Testament experience, we discovered what happens when we don't rest: We miss out on the blessings of a whole life.

WHOLE LIFE CHALLENGE

At the close of the chapter, I challenged you to carve out times of rest in your life on a daily basis with proper sleep, on a weekly basis with a Sabbath day, and on a quarterly basis with a retreat.

What do you need to change to make rest a priority in your Whole Life rhythm? I encourage you to make sure you are getting adequate sleep each night. If you're not, adjust your schedule accordingly, removing unnecessary activities that keep you from getting to bed early enough and making adjustments in your bedroom to encourage sleep: a comfortable mattress, proper window coverings, and soft lighting. If these simple solutions don't result in better sleep, schedule a consultation with your doctor.

Take a look at your calendar and choose a weekly and quarterly time to rest. Which day of the week works best with your work schedule and other commitments to set aside as a Sabbath? If that day is Saturday or Sunday and allows you to attend services at your church, great. If not, pick another day and keep it clear on your calendar. Put these findings in a journal for reflection and on your calendar to keep you consistent.

For your quarterly rest, plan a retreat. Research options that will fit your budget and lifestyle and allow you to get away from your house or city in order to recharge and refocus on God. Pick a tentative date for your retreat and get excited for some well-earned time away. Again, write your quarterly plans for this calendar year down in your journal and schedule them on your calendar or agenda.

Completing these challenges in the area of rest is sure to increase your score on your Whole Life Wheel and bring about greater stamina, greater clarity, and even greater trust in God.

Conclusion

As you come to the end of this book, I congratulate you on taking your initial step toward bettering yourself by finding God's rhythm for your whole life. The fact that you have gotten to the conclusion means that you have learned a lot of information on the way to help you improve your spirit, soul, and body. Below you will find the Whole Life Wheel. My intention behind inserting it again at the end of the book is to give you an opportunity to measure yourself and compare your results to those at the beginning of the book.

If you read this book from cover to cover without starting the process, I encourage you to wait to fill out the new wheel until after you have had a few weeks to add some of these principles to your life and schedule. If you have a busy schedule like I did, know that I'm praying for you so that you can carve out the time needed to apply the principles presented in this book.

Before you start, remember the encouragement from verse 24 of 1 Thessalonians 5 that "the one who calls you is faithful, and he will do it." I believe as you set your heart to begin your journey toward wholeness that God has already grabbed you by the hand and will lead you into the rhythm that works for your life. There will be some discouraging days; I have had many in my journey. However, I know that with His help He will lead you to a place of health and wholeness greater than you have ever known.

I have by no means achieved perfection in my Whole Life rhythm. Day after day, week after week, I'm still tweaking here and there as the Lord leads me. Even though I am much closer today, I remind you that the goal of this book has never been to reach a place of perfection. We will all reach that place someday, when we meet the Lord in heaven. But until then give yourself lots of grace on your journey toward a whole life and allow yourself to enjoy the process of discovering what works for you.

Before you fill out your new Whole Life Wheel, take a moment to revisit the nine developmental areas we covered in this book, as outlined below.

Spiritual Formation

P = Prayer. I have a vibrant prayer life and hear from God regularly.

B = Bible reading. I am regularly reading and applying God's Word to my life.

D = Dream. I am walking toward God's dream for my life.

Soul Care

M = Mind. My thoughts about God, myself, and others line up with Scripture.

W = Will. My will is in line with what I believe God's priorities are for my life.

E = Emotion. My emotions are healthy and submitted to my mind and will.

Body Health

N = Nutrition. I am eating nutritiously, hydrating frequently, and taking any needed supplements.

F = Fitness. I am in good physical health and exercising at least three times a week.

R = Rest. I am creating space in my life for daily, weekly, and quarterly rest.

When you finish filling in the wheel, compare your most recent ratings with those from your wheel at the beginning of the book

(p. 13). In which areas have you grown? Does your current wheel look any more roadworthy than the first one?

Practical application of truth is what brings genuine transformation in your life. If you began to implement some of the challenges at the end of each chapter to your life, great! Continue to build on what you have already done, and you will continue to grow. If you weren't able to take me up on the challenges, a good way to get a jump start is to go back and focus on one or two of your weakest areas and complete the Whole Life challenge for those chapters. Remember, this process should not be difficult but rather life-giving. Therefore, it's important to come up with a plan that helps you have fun while achieving your goals in the process.

THE WHOLE LIFE PLAN

As a supplement to this book, I have added a section at the end of this conclusion called the Whole Life Plan. This plan is essentially a culmination of the Whole Life challenges at the end of each chapter. This plan will serve as a template for you to have all of your findings in one easy-to-find location. Since the goal of this book is for you to create a lifestyle of rhythm in all parts of yourself—spirit, soul, and body—it is also a great opportunity to complete any of the Whole Life challenges that you may have missed within the chapters. By having this information all in one spot, it is sure to provide an effective reference until you make this plan a part of your lifestyle.

Since most people don't give these areas much thought without prompting, this will prove to be a valuable exercise as you create a realistic plan for your own life. Remember, it's important to develop a lifestyle plan that is realistic for you. There is no competition here. As you carve out time to complete this plan, be sure to say a quick prayer and ask God to guide you into things that will really work for you. With His help, you are sure to come up with a grace-filled Whole Life Plan that will stick.

Start with the foundation of your spiritual formation: regular time spent with God and His Word. If this was already a regular part of your life before reading this book, how has your understanding of prayer and the Word increased? Since many of the other challenges in the book require you to ask God for direction, wisdom, or a plan, make sure you are regularly speaking to Him and allowing Him to speak to you through His Word. Have you figured out the next steps in your dream?

I hope that the condition of your soul was not as messy as mine was, but realistically I know many people could probably relate to the insights shared in the mind, will, and emotion chapters. If you have dealt with the ungodly beliefs that I shared in chapter five, have you replaced yours with godly beliefs and support scriptures? Remember that repetition is the key once you have identified your new godly beliefs. I still go back over mine on a regular basis just to refresh my mind. If you are ever having a bad day or find yourself lacking in confidence, pull out those godly beliefs.

Have you sought out relationships—a Whole Life partner, a small group at your local church, or close Christian friends—to share your goals with and keep you accountable and encouraged as you integrate Whole Life principles into your life? Next to your communication with the Lord, these relationships will be key to your success, offering you a place to process what you are learning and feeling. Some of the greatest joy we will experience on earth will be with the individuals whom we call family and friends, and pursuing a whole life is no exception to that truth.

And last but not least, think about how your body has changed during this journey. Whether you needed to work on nutrition, fitness, or rest, I hope you have been able to set some concrete goals that you can work toward. This area can be the most difficult for many, but growth in it will positively affect your soul and spirit as a by-product. Remember, your body is the temple of the Holy Spirit, and proper stewardship of your body will give you the strength, stamina, and focus to be able to walk out God's purpose for your life.

As I said earlier in the book, Paul's words in 1 Thessalonians 5:23 were to believers like you and me. They were a prayer for the Thessalonian believers that we can apply to our lives. My prayer for you is that God will give you the grace to practically apply these Whole Life principles to your life, and as you do, that *the God of peace Himself sanctify you completely, and may your whole spirit and soul and body be kept blameless at the coming of our Lord Jesus Christ.*

The promise I made at the beginning of the book holds true here at the end. Your issues may not be the same as mine, but by taking stock of where you are on the journey to wholeness, committing to change, and applying the principles found in even one or two of these chapters, you, too, can see the same results as I have: restoration in your emotions, clarity in your mind, fresh strength in your body, and a reinvigorated relationship with God.

Enjoy your new, whole life!

THE WHOLE LIFE PLAN

SPIRITUAL FORMATION:

Prayer: (List your current prayer requests.)

1. ....
2. ....
3. ....

Bible: (Describe your chosen Bible study plan.)

....

....

....

Dream: (List your top three dreams for this current season.)

1. ....
2. ....
3. ....

SOUL CARE:

Mind: (List three godly beliefs.)

1. ....
2. ....
3. ....

Will: (List your valued priorities.)

1. ....
2. ....
3. ....
4. ....
5. ....

Emotions: (List your three close Christian friends.)

1. ....

2. ....

3. ....

BODY HEALTH:

Nutrition:

Weight goal:

....

Eating plan or diet:

....

Glasses of water per day:

....

Fitness:

Describe your workout plan:

....

Goal event:

....

Rest:

How many hours of sleep will you get a night?

....

What day will your Sabbath be on?

....

List your quarterly retreat dates over the next 12 months:

1. ....

2. ....

3. ....

4. ....

Acknowledgments

Thanks be to God, as the initial idea for this book started way back in 2002 while I was sitting in a seminary class, daydreaming. Thank you for all the inspiration along the way, Lord.

To my wife, Taryn, you somehow lived the Whole Life message before it was even a concept in my mind. Thank you for modeling the Whole Life to me so that I could see it in you and eventually write this book. I love you.

To my children. Many years from now I want you all to read this book, as the principles contained in it will keep you healthy and vibrant for all of your days so that you can achieve all God has dreamed for you. Thank you for being the main inspiration that I had in making the Whole Life my personal journey. I love you all.

To my mom and dad: Thanks for believing in me when I was still yet to be believable. I love you.

To my dear friend Matthew Stroia: Thanks for being a friend who is "closer than a brother."

To Metro Church and staff: Thank you for allowing me to be your pastor for ten years. It was one of the greatest seasons of my life. Thanks also for allowing me to test these Whole Life concepts on you first. Without your support and excitement about this subject, it would not have culminated in a book. You all mean the world to me.

A special thank you to Jay Bruce, Becka Gruber, Tiffany Johnson, and Julie Reams. You four ladies have such a way of making projects come alive, and I loved working with you on my initial attempt to finish this book.

To my friend and literary agent, Cassie Hanjian: You are such a wonderful person and I am so thankful that God had our paths cross so many years ago. Thank you for always championing whatever I dream up to write about. You are such an encourager.

To my publisher, Howard Books, and especially Beth Adams: Thank you for redeeming this book. At one point I did not think it would ever be published. Thank you for believing in this message and in me.

To my friend David Yeazell: This makes four books (technically) that we have worked on together. Thank you for your undying support for whatever I dream up to write about.

To my friends Jeff Johnson and Kurt Wachle: Thank you for helping me to further reach my fitness goals through the weight-loss tips and ideas that both of you have shared with me. These tips were so helpful, but not nearly as much as both of your inspirational stories.

To my friend and business partner, Richard Matthews: Thank you for helping me to turn this material into an amazing online course.

Appendix—Chapter Resources

Chapter Three: Bible—A Gift from Above
Two online Bible study resources that I recommend are Biblestudytools
.com and Biblegateway.com.

Chapter Four: Dream—Discovering Your Purpose
Below is a free online spiritual gifts test:

Spiritualgiftstest.com

Some other resources for spiritual gifts:

Discover Your Spiritual Gifts by C. Peter Wagner
Finding Your Spiritual Gifts by C. Peter Wagner

Chapter Eight: Nutrition—You Are What You Eat
Below are a few of the many diet plans available:

DASH Eating Plan
The DASH Diet (government-endorsed and ranked #1 in diets by *U.S. News & World Report*) is effective in both preventing and lowering high blood pressure (hypertension). This diet emphasizes eating all of the foods we know are good for us—fruits, veggies, whole grains, lean protein, and low-fat dairy—and shuns all of the calorie- and fat-packed sweets and red meats that we love to indulge in.
www.dashforhealth.com[1]

Therapeutic Lifestyle Changes (TLC) Eating Plan
The Therapeutic Lifestyle Changes Diet is known to cut high cholesterol. The American Heart Association has also endorsed this diet as a healthy-heart regimen that can reduce the risk of cardiovascular disease. The TLC diet cuts away saturated fats such as fried foods, whole milk, and fatty meats; and promotes the consumption of fiber.
https://www.nhlbi.nih.gov/files/docs/public/heart/chol_tlc.pdf[2]

Whole30 Eating Plan

For thirty days you cut all sugar, alcohol, grains, dairy, and legumes from your diet—elements known to contribute to several common physical and mental health issues, including allergies, acne, and depression. By doing so, you basically reprogram your body—and taste buds—and find freedom from poor eating habits and unhealthy thought patterns associated with food.

whole30.com[3]

Mediterranean Eating Plan

The Mediterranean Diet is aimed at weight loss. This diet stems from a study that shows that people bordering the Mediterranean Sea not only suffer less from ailments common to most Americans but also live longer. The Mediterranean Diet promotes an active lifestyle as well as a diet low in red meat, sugar, and saturated fat. Aside from weight loss, this diet helps to avoid a host of chronic diseases.

www.mayoclinic.org/healthy-lifestyle/nutrition-and-healthy-eating /in-depth/mediterranean-diet/art-20047801[4]

The Flexitarian Eating Plan

The Flexitarian Diet promotes optimal health. This diet combines being both *flexible* and *vegetarian*, promoting a healthy balance between vegetables and meats—including having the occasional burger or steak whenever you get the urge! Flexitarians are known to have a lower rate of heart disease, diabetes, and cancer.

health.usnews.com/best-diet/flexitarian-diet[5]
dawnjacksonblatner.com/books/the-flexitarian-diet/[6]

Wheat Belly Eating Plan

The Wheat Belly Diet manages blood sugar levels and promotes weight loss through the elimination of all wheat-based products and sugary-based products such as bread, cereal, pasta, and soda. It also encourages the consumption of fresh, unprocessed produce and nuts. The Wheat Belly Diet is known to reduce heart disease and diabetes.

www.wheatbelly.com[7]

The Fast Eating Plan

The Fast Diet is based on intermittent fasting and can easily be remembered by one term: 5:2—five days of normal eating, and two days of reduced-calorie eating. This diet promotes weight loss by reducing the amount you eat for short periods of time. Studies reveal that the

Fast Diet has a wide range of health benefits, including improvements in blood pressure and cholesterol levels.
thefastdiet.co.uk[8]

Mayo Clinic Eating Plan

The Mayo Clinic Diet promotes both rapid and long-term weight loss. This diet begins with a two-week period, Phase One, where five bad habits are replaced with five good habits. Most people lose between 6 and 10 pounds during this phase. The remainder of the diet, Phase Two, is based on a combination of portion control and physical activity. Most people lose 2 to 3 pounds a week during this phase.
diet.mayoclinic.org[9]

South Beach Eating Plan

The South Beach Diet is a healthy approach to eating that can help jump-start weight loss and lower cholesterol. This diet is composed of three steps that eliminate specific items from your diet, like sugary foods and refined starches, and gradually adds them back in healthy moderation while helping you maintain a goal weight. The South Beach diet is popular for its practical and fast results.
www.southbeachdiet.com[10]

21-Day Eating Plan

The 21-Day Diet was created around the idea that it takes twenty-one days to successfully create a habit. This diet combines portion control with regular physical activity to promote weight loss in three weeks. At the beginning, you determine your calorie intake needed to lose weight. The 21-Day Diet also introduces color-coded containers to weekly meal planning: Each colored container represents a vegetable, protein, fruit, or carb. On average, most people following the 21-Day Diet will lose 15 pounds in three weeks.
www.daystofitness.com[11]

The Maker's Diet

The Maker's Diet is built on principles found throughout the Bible and takes forty days to complete. This diet is rich in whole, organic foods. It includes red meats, carbs, and small portions of saturated fats, and excludes all processed foods. This diet is known to remove toxins that can cause other health issues within our bodies, and aims to help people achieve and maintain overall wellness.
makersdiet.com[12]

Below is a link to all of the Whole Life supplements and multivitamins:

The Whole Life Supplements
www.thewholelife.store

Chapter Nine: Fitness—Decide. Commit. Succeed.
To download Tony Horton's specific plan, go to Beachbody.com. I also encourage you to check out Tony's large selection of books and videos on the subject of fitness as well as nutrition. Besides Tony's program, Beachbody.com has a wide variety of video trainers you can check out.

You can download Krista Stryker's app and view demonstrations of the exercises included in this book at www.12minuteahtlete.com.

Some healthy fast-food and chain restaurant low-calorie meal options:[13]

- ✦ McDonald's, Egg McMuffin (300 calories)
- ✦ Arby's, Turkey Gyro (470 calories)
- ✦ KFC, 3 Piece Grilled Chicken with Green Beans (465 calories)
- ✦ Taco Bell, Veggie Power Bowl (480 calories)
- ✦ Popeyes, 3-Piece Blackened Chicken Tenders with Green Beans (225 calories)
- ✦ Sonic, Classic Grilled Chicken Sandwich (460 calories)
- ✦ Chili's, Sirloin with Grilled Avocado (420 calories)
- ✦ Noodles & Co., Japanese Pan Noodles (330 calories)
- ✦ Red Robin, Wedgie Burger (430 calories)
- ✦ IHOP, Simple & Fit 2-Egg Breakfast (400 calories)
- ✦ TGI Fridays, Bourbon Barrel Chicken with Tomato Mozzarella Salad (380 calories)
- ✦ Red Lobster, Garlic-Grilled Shrimp (350 calories)
- ✦ Applebee's, Thai Shrimp Salad (390 calories)
- ✦ Chick-fil-A, 8-Piece Grilled Nuggets with a Superfood Side (330 calories)
- ✦ Dairy Queen, Chicken BLT Salad (270 Calories)

David's favorite food choices:

Breakfast:

- ✦ Chobani yogurt (plain)
- ✦ Greek yogurt
- ✦ Eggs
- ✦ Instant Oatmeal
- ✦ Honey Nut Cheerios
- ✦ Fat-free milk
- ✦ Bananas
- ✦ Cottage cheese
- ✦ Turkey or chicken deli meat

Lunch:

- ✦ Chili
- ✦ Grilled chicken
- ✦ Deli meats, turkey and chicken
- ✦ Barbecue chicken (all white meat)
- ✦ Lima beans (high protein)
- ✦ Baked beans (high protein)
- ✦ Black beans (high protein)
- ✦ Spinach salad
- ✦ Cottage cheese
- ✦ Cherry tomatoes
- ✦ Peas (high protein)
- ✦ Chik-fil-A Char Grilled Sandwich
- ✦ Chik-fil-A Grilled Nuggets
- ✦ Lean ground beef
- ✦ Low-fat milk

Dinner:

- ✦ Filet mignon
- ✦ Sushi (tuna or salmon)
- ✦ Steamed veggies
- ✦ Pork tenderloin

- Ahi tuna
- Salads with grilled chicken (be careful with the dressing)
- Chili
- Beans
- Edamame
- Tuna poke
- Shrimp cocktail

Snacks:

- Beef jerky
- Tootsie Rolls (10 calories each)
- Smarties (10 calories each)
- Dark chocolate
- Pretzels
- Apples
- Oranges
- Pure protein bars
- Pure protein shakes (chocolate)
- Dark chocolate almonds (Trader Joe's)
- Muscle Milk (100-calorie version)
- Low-calorie ice cream

Notes

Chapter 1: A Life Lived Whole

1. King James Version (KJV).
2. Lewis, C. S. *Mere Christianity* (London: Collins, 1952), pp. 54–56. (In all editions, this is Book II, Chapter 3, "The Shocking Alternative.")
3. Buseck, Craig. "The Three Parts of Man," CBN.com. www1.cbn.com/ questions/what-are-the-three-parts-of-man.
4. King James Version (KJV).

PART ONE: SPIRITUAL FORMATION

1. Fletcher, Dale. "Wholeness—A Biblical and Christian Perspective." FaithandHealthConnection.org, www.faithandhealthconnection.org/ the_connection/spirit-soul-and-body/wholeness-biblical-and-christian -perspective/.
2. Fletcher, Dale. "Spirit, Soul and Body—How God Designed Us." FaithandHealthConnection.org, www.faithandhealthconnection.org/ the_connection/spirit-soul-and-body.
3. www.dwillard.org/articles/artview.

Chapter 2: Prayer—The Secret to a Powerful Life

1. Quote commonly attributed to Saint Francis of Assisi.
2. Tozer, A.W. *The Pursuit of God* (Abbotsford, WI: Aneko Press, Life Sentence Publishing, 2015), Chapter 4.
3. Ibid.
4. Lawrence, Brother. *The Practice of the Presence of God*, Conrad De-Meester, ed., and Salvatore Sciurba, trans. (Washington, DC: ICS Publications, 1994).
5. Johnson, Bill. *The Supernatural Power of a Transformed Mind* (Shippensburg, PA: Destiny Image, 2005).
6. New Living Translation (NLT).
7. Quote attributed to Charles Spurgeon.
8. Foster, Richard J. *Celebration of Discipline: The Path to Spiritual Growth*, 3rd ed. (San Francisco: HarperOne, 1998).

Chapter 3: Bible—A Gift from Above

1. Radosh, Daniel. "The Good Book Business," *New Yorker*, December 18, 2006. www.newyorker.com/magazine/2006/12/18/the-good-book-business.
2. Bell, Caleb K. "Poll: Americans Love the Bible but Don't Read It Much," Religion News Service, April 4, 2013. www.religionnews.com/2013/04/04/poll-americans-love-the-bible-but-dont-read-it-much/.

Chapter 4: Dream—Discovering Your Purpose

1. King, Martin Luther Jr. "I Have a Dream" (1963), in *Let Nobody Turn Us Around: Voices of Resistance, Reform, and Renewal: An African American Anthology,* Manning Marable and Leith Mullings, eds. (Lanham, MD: Rowman & Littlefield, 1999).
2. Rath, Tom. *Strengths Finder 2.0* (New York: Gallup Press, 2007).
3. ten Boom, Corrie, with Elizabeth and John Sherrill. *The Hiding Place* (Grand Rapids, MI: Chosen, 2006), p. 12.

PART TWO: SOUL CARE

Chapter 5: Mind—A Beautiful Mind

1. Young's Literal Translation (YLT).
2. Kylstra, Chester, and Betsy Kylstra. *Restoring the Foundations* (Proclaiming His Word, Inc., 2001), p. 157.
3. www.restoringthefoundations.uk.
4. Kylstra, Chester, and Betsy Kylstra, *Restoring the Foundations,* p. 353.
5. Wilson, Sandra D. *Released from Shame: Moving Beyond the Pain of the Past* (Downers Grove, IL: Inter-Varsity Press, 2003).
6. New American Standard Bible (NASB).
7. Mounce Reverse-Interlinear New Testament (MOUNCE).
8. Field, T. A., E. T. Beeson, and L. K. Jones. *The New ABCs: A Practitioner's Guide to Neuroscience-Informed Cognitive Behavioral Therapy* (PDF), *Journal of Mental Health Counseling* 37, no. 3 (2015), pp. 206–20.
9. New Living Translation (NLT).

Chapter 6: Will—It's Your Choice

1. "1343. dikaiosuné," BibleHub.com. http://biblehub.com/greek/1343.htm.

Chapter 7: Emotions—He Restores My Soul

1. "Definition of Echo," Merriam-Webster.com. www.merriam-webster.com/dictionary/echo.
2. New American Standard Bible (NASB).
3. Ibid.
4. Grueneich, Myron. "Upside Down Time . . ." Life in the Sheep Pen (blog), WordPress, July 15, 2010. https://hissheep.wordpress.com/2010/07/15/upside-down-time/.

5. Good News Translation (GNT).
6. GOD'S WORD translation (GW).
7. Phillips, Donald T. *Martin Luther King, Jr., on Leadership*, reissue edition (New York: Warner Books, 2000).
8. Ibid.
9. Mandela, Nelson. Goodreads.com. www.goodreads.com/quotes/144557 -resentment-is-like-drinking-poison-and-then-hoping-it-will.
10. New Living Translation (NLT).
11. Keller, Timothy. *Prayer* (New York: Penguin Books, 2016), p. 228.
12. SubstanceChurch.com,https://substancechurch.com/wp-content/uploads /2016/03/QA-ChurchSize2016.pdf.
13. Lunden, Joan, "Why Friends Are Even More Important as We Age," *Today* video, May 24, 2016. Today.com, www.today.com/video/why -friends-are-even-more-important-as-we-age-691688003521.

PART THREE: BODY HEALTH

Chapter 8: Nutrition—You Are What You Eat

1. Horton, Tony, "How to Eat More and Lose Weight," Beach Body on Demand (blog), July 3, 2015. www.beachbodyondemand.com/blog/eat-more-and-lose-weight (Be sure to scroll down the page to the article.) Quoted with permission from the author.
2. Osterweil, Neil. "The Benefits of Protein." Webmd.com, WebMD, LLC (2017).
3. Harvard, T. H. Chan School of Public Health, *The Nutrition Source* (2017), The President and Fellows of Harvard College.
4. Kannall, Erica. "What Are Lipids Used for in the Body?" http://healthy eating.sfgate.com/lipids-used-body-8282.html.
5. Horton, Tony, "Water vs. Coke," Tony Horton's Blog Spot, blogpot.com, February 4, 2008. http://tonyhorton.blogspot.com/2008/02/water-vs -coke.html. (Quoted with permission from the author.)
6. Ibid.
7. Ibid.
8. Ibid.
9. Ibid.
10. Mohan, Carmen Patrick. "The Facts on Omega-3 Fatty Acids," WebMD Medical Reference, webmd.com, May 18, 2017.
11. Faye, Denis. "Tony Horton's Four Must-Have Supplements," Nutrition Nerd, denisfaye.com, February 4, 2014. http://denisfaye.com/2014/02/04/ tony-hortons-four-must-have-supplements/. (Quoted with permission from the author.)
12. Ibid.
13. Ibid.

14. *Courtney, Emily,* "How Probiotics Detoxify Your Gut Environment." www
     .hyperbiotics.com/blogs/recent-articles/how-probiotics-detoxify
     -your-gut-environment.
15. "Key Recommendations: Components of Healthy Eating Patterns," *2014–
     2020 Dietary Guidelines,* health.gov. https://health.gov/dietaryguide
     lines/2015/guidelines/chapter-1/key-recommendations/.

Chapter 9: Fitness—Decide. Commit. Succeed.

1. Barnes, Albert. "Commentary on 1 Corinthians 9:27." "Barnes' Notes on
    the New Testament." https://www.studylight.org/commentaries/bnb
    /1-corinthians-9.html. 1870.
2. Ibid.
3. Reynolds, Gretchen. "The Scientific 7-Minute Workout," *New York Times,*
    May 12, 2013, p. 20.
4. Lliades, Charles, MD. "Why You Need Aerobic Exercise," Everyday
    Health.com. www.everydayhealth.com/fitness/workouts/why-you-need
    -aerobic-exercise.aspx.
5. Gustafson, Kristin. "5 Benefits of Weight Training," Active.com. www
    .active.com/fitness/articles/5-benefits-of-weight-training.
6. "Benefits if Anaerobic Exercise," HealthStatus.com. www.healthstatus
    .com/health_blog/plan-for-weight-loss/benefits-anaerobic-exercise/.
7. Castro, Cynthia M., and Abby C. King. "Stanford University 24 Years of
    Research on Phone Coaching for Physical Activity," FitnessByPhone
    .com. www.fitnessbyphone.com/stanford.html.
8. http://blog.codyapp.com/2013/07/30/workout-partner-motivation
    -exercises/.
9. Beach Body, LLC.

Chapter 10: Rest—Recreate, Recharge, and Refocus

1. New American Standard Bible (NASB).
2. New Living Translation (NLT).
3. New Century Version (NCV).
4. English Standard Version (ESV).
5. Ramsey, Dave. *The Total Money Makeover: A Proven Plan for Financial
    Fitness.* Nashville, TN.: Nelson, 2013.
6. New Century Version (NCV).
7. New American Standard Bible (NASB).
8. Ibid.
9. English Standard Version (ESV).
10. *rest,* Dictionary.com. http://dictionary.reference.com/browse/rest?s=t.
11. "Introduction to Daniel's Seventy Weeks," JewishRoots.net. www.jewishroots
    .net/library/prophecy/daniel/daniel-9-24-27/introduction-to-daniel-9
    -24-27-prophecy.html.

12. National Sleep Foundation, "How Much Sleep Do We Really Need?" sleepfoundation.org. https://sleepfoundation.org/how-sleep-works/how -much-sleep-do-we-really-need/page/0/2.

Appendix—Chapter Resources

1. DASH for Health, dashforhealth.com. www.dashforhealth.com/?gclid =CMyky92ezs0CFUpZhgodpWcJuw.
2. National Heart, Lung, and Blood Institute, "Your Guide to Lower-ing Your Cholesterol with TLC" (PDF). www.nhlbi.nih.gov/files/docs/ public/heart/chol_tlc.pdf.
3. "The Official Whole 30 Program Rules," whole30.com. http://whole30 .com/whole30-program-rules/.
4. Mayo Clinic Staff, "Mediterranean Diet: A Heart-Healthy Eating Plan," Mayoclinic.org. www.mayoclinic.org/healthy-lifestyle/nutrition-and-healthy -eating/in-depth/mediterranean-diet/art-20047801.
5. "Best Diets: The Flexitarian Diet," *U.S. News and World Report*, health .usnews.com. http://health.usnews.com/best-diet/flexitarian-diet.
6. https://dawnjacksonblatner.com/books/the-flexitarian-diet/.
7. Wheat Belly Lifestyle Institute. www.wheatbelly.com/.
8. The 5:2 Fast Diet. https://thefastdiet.co.uk/.
9. The Mayo Clinic Diet. http://diet.mayoclinic.org/diet/home.
10. South Beach Diet. www.southbeachdiet.com/diet/.
11. Sarah, "The 21 Day Fix Eating Plan," daysoffitness.com. www.daysto fitness.com/21-day-fix-eating-plan/.
12. Rubin, Jordan. The Maker's Diet. www.ncbi.nlm.nih.gov/pubmed/8775648.
13. Calderone, Ann, and Shay Spence. "The Healthiest Meals to Order at Fast Food and Chain Restaurants," *People*, January 11, 2018.